D0500096

PRAISE FOR *MY RESCUE DOG RESCUED ME*

"We commend this book for sharing some wonderful stories of how rescuing a dog from a shelter can not only transform the life of that dog but also the lives of those who adopt them. We rescue some of the worst cases of animal abuse, and seeing how these dogs learn to forgive and trust humans again is an example we can learn from. You can't buy love but you can rescue it." —Soi Dog Foundation

"A gorgeous book showing the incredible power of the relationship between human and dog and how it can change lives for those with four legs and two. An absolute must-read for anyone who's known the incomparable love of a rescue dog. Waggy tails all round for Sharon Ward Keeble's charming, heartwarming book." —*YOURS* magazine

"Keeble has, in this great collection of stories, managed to capture the unconditional devotion dogs continue to give us all despite an often harsh beginning in life. Whether it be a local rescue or one from a war-torn country, the undaunted loyalty and love remains the same." —War Paws charity

"A fantastic celebration of rescue dogs and the capacity they have to change lives. . . . it drives home the message that you really should Adopt Not Shop. If you are not convinced, just read some of the heartwarming stories, and try not to cry." —Spanish Stray Dogs charity

"This book has character and heart. It illustrates the power of human and animal relationships. It's touching and informative, and helps us understand our canine companions even more. It is a must-read for dog lovers, but also for anyone whose life has been touched by an animal, and knows the comfort and joy they can bring." —*Take a Break* magazine

"*My Rescue Dog Rescued Me* is full of heartwarming tales of rags-to-riches Rovers who have become heroes to their humans." —*Real People* magazine

Copyright © 2017 by Sharon Ward Keeble
First published by Summersdale Publishers Ltd., © 2016

Skyhorse Publishing books may be purchased in bulk at special discounts for sales promotion, corporate gifts, fund-raising, or educational purposes. Special editions can also be created to specifications. For details, contact the Special Sales Department, Skyhorse Publishing, 307 West 36th Street, 11th Floor, New York, NY 10018 or info@skyhorsepublishing.com.

Skyhorse® and Skyhorse Publishing® are registered trademarks of Skyhorse Publishing, Inc.®, a Delaware corporation.

Visit our website at www.skyhorsepublishing.com.

10 9 8 7 6 5 4 3 2 1

Library of Congress Cataloging-in-Publication Data is available on file.

Print ISBN: 978-1-5107-1737-4
Ebook ISBN: 978-1-5107-1738-1

Printed in the United States of America

My Rescue Dog Rescued Me

Amazing true stories of adopted canine heroes

Sharon Ward Keeble

Skyhorse Publishing

To my own rescue dogs, Beau and Alfie

*Thank you both for all the love and happiness
you give to me and our family*

*You have both shown us what unconditional
love really means, and by doing so you have
been my inspiration to write this book*

ABOUT THE AUTHOR

Sharon Ward Keeble is a journalist with more than 20 years' experience of national reporting for major women's magazines and newspapers in the UK and USA, including *Closer*, *Bella* and the *Sunday Mirror*. She is the author of *China: Passport to Adventure* and co-author of *The Horse Girl*. She is based in Florida.

CONTENTS

INTRODUCTION

There have been only a few times in my life when I haven't had a four-legged friend to keep me company, but I've grown up with a very particular and very special kind of dog: rescue dogs. My parents rescued animals from shelters rather than buy from breeders and I learned from an early age that dogs from these backgrounds, despite their previous experiences, can prove themselves to be the most loyal of pets.

However, it wasn't until my daughter Molly was bullied at school and we adopted a dog, a sandy-coloured terrier she called Alfie, that I really appreciated what these special animals can teach us. By witnessing the unique bond that Molly and Alfie formed, I realised that although we rescued this pup from a shelter, it was Alfie who truly rescued my daughter from the trauma of bullying.

While researching this book, I came across countless inspiring stories which demonstrate the extent to which adopted dogs give back to their new families. These incredible canines provide much-needed physical and emotional support – a stroke of the head or a long-lasting hug can make all the difference to an owner suffering from illness or distress deep within their souls – and some of these dogs have even become lifesavers. Turn the pages to meet Brin, the flea-bitten dog rescued from war-torn Afghanistan to live with Sally, a lupus sufferer, in England. And then there is the cheeky little terrier who transformed the sad life of his widowed owner; a fearless St Bernard dog named Hercules; and the memorable tale of a dog who performed the Heimlich manoeuvre...

Too many people won't even consider adopting dogs from shelters because they dismiss them as 'damaged'. This book is a celebration of the rescue dogs who turn the tables around and save their human owners. My hope is that it will encourage people to adopt a dog (rather than shop for one) because the rescued breed is quite simply the most loyal and charming you will find.

although we rescued this pup from a shelter, it was Alfie who truly rescued my daughter

CHAPTER 1

BEVERLI AND PIPER'S STORY

Beverli felt as though her life was charmed and considered herself an incredibly lucky person. The consultancy firm she worked for had just helped London win its bid to host the 2012 Olympic Games. Part of a team of highly skilled professionals, Beverli's job was to oversee and devise practical solutions for matters relating to the potential terrorism that such a prestigious event would attract.

Her area of expertise was security, and in particular the security of the hard and soft rings, the competitive arenas within the Olympic city, and the tagging of athletes to ensure the safety of the world's top sportspeople. As she boarded the Tube train at King's Cross Station in London, it was time to get down to business after the celebratory party the night before. Beverli, full of excitement and anticipation, couldn't wait to get to work on starting a new chapter in her career. As she hopped onto the train at

8.42 a.m., she was already planning the safety measures that she was going to recommend to her bosses that morning.

It was a tight squeeze in the train but somehow Beverli managed to get a seat. Just before the train was due to stop at Russell Square, where she had to get off, she stood up and held on to the metal rail until the train came to a halt. Suddenly, there was an excruciating sound of metal grating against metal as the train screeched to a stop. Beverli was flung forward and hit the pole face-first with such force that it knocked her out.

The next thing she knew, she was lying on the floor. From looking at her watch, she worked out that she had been like that for about twelve and a half minutes. She couldn't hear anything apart from a high-pitched ringing in her ears.

Thick black smoke filled the carriage and she could barely breathe, although she could make out shadowy figures in the train. The high-pitched noise was replaced with people screaming and shouting for help.

'It was chaos,' recalls Beverli. 'People didn't know what had happened, but I did – I realised a bomb had gone off. I'd lived in South Africa, where guerilla warfare was a normal part of life and bombs would go off in public places every day. I knew it was a bomb.'

After the explosion, the lights had gone out and the emergency lights in the train carriage had been activated, but they appeared only faintly because of the thick black smoke billowing everywhere. Beverli got on her hands and knees and crawled along the floor in the direction she thought the doors might be but, as she moved along, she was aware of a warm, spongy feeling in her face and mouth.

'I didn't know it, but there was blood pouring down my face from where I'd hit the metal pole,' says Beverli. 'I had lost most of my teeth and the ones I did have left were on the bottom jaw wedged into my gums. My chest felt like I had been whacked there with a baseball bat several times and the whole left side of my face and body felt as if it was on fire. I was in pain but not as much as you might have expected with such horrific injuries – the adrenalin must have kicked in. The sound of people screaming will live with me forever. Some were badly injured or dying; others were terrified; and others were freaking out because it was so black and smoky down there. It was how I imagined hell.'

With a strength that she didn't know she possessed, Beverli stayed calm and made getting out of the mangled train carriage her focus. She took a woman's hand and they struggled to stand up together. They picked their way through the passengers, trying desperately not to tread on anybody as they brushed past warm bodies – some moving, others slumped against the seats or the carriage walls.

Blood was dripping down Beverli's face like water and, for a moment, she wondered if she was going to die in there, on the day that turned out to be the UK's worst ever terrorist attack: the 7 July 2005 London bombings.

One passenger had found the emergency exit and he pushed it open, so Beverli and a handful of others managed to get out of the carriage and onto the power lines. They had no idea if the tracks were live, but they had to take the chance or they faced being burned alive.

Together the group staggered through the Underground tunnel towards the next station. It was so dark and musty down there that they had to grope their way along the old tiled walls, which felt cold and smooth. The smell was musky like an old nightclub, making Beverli gag as she walked.

The scene when they eventually reached the next station was of utter chaos. There were paramedics, firefighters and police everywhere, helping the injured and dying; terrified people trying to make phone calls or just screaming with fear. It was like a scene out of a movie, only it wasn't a movie – it was all too real.

Beverli managed to get to a hospital while London was on lockdown. A major terrorist cell had planned four separate bombings in the capital within the space of minutes, maiming thousands and killing many. It was the blackest of days for the UK.

The event dramatically changed the course of Beverli's life. 'Up until this moment in my life, I don't know if I had ever felt happier,' she muses. 'My life felt pretty much mapped out and I liked the certainty. I was living in London with my long-term partner Tina in a beautiful house; I had amazing friends and a fabulous job. Life was good and I had such high expectations for my future. As I stood on the King's Cross

Station platform that morning, it seemed extra crowded with lots of commuters and tourists going about their business. I'd felt so lucky to be a part of the London life. It was a good one.'

Beverli's recovery was long and slow. Part of her face had been smashed in and she had swallowed toxic chemicals in the tunnel. Additionally, she had suffered a concussion to her head and minor brain damage from hitting the metal pole in the carriage.

I felt like my life was over

'The brain damage left me with minor memory and speech problems, but the doctors said I should be grateful to have survived at all,' recalls Beverli. 'Over the next few years, I had many painful surgeries to rebuild my face and my mouth. I couldn't work. I couldn't do anything normal any more. I felt like my life was over.'

Beverli suffered severe post-traumatic stress disorder (PTSD) – for her, this condition was far worse to deal with than the surgeries. For months, she couldn't set foot out of her front door for fear that something would happen to her. She developed survivor's guilt, because she couldn't understand why *she* had lived when so many others died. Even sleep offered no respite as she experienced horrific dreams in which she relived the bombings.

Beverli underwent a lot of therapy, which was helpful to an extent. However, every time she heard a police or ambulance siren, she would run or hold her head in her hands to drown out the noise because she associated it with that fateful day. If it wasn't for her partner holding her while she screamed and cried all night, she wouldn't have made it through.

'Tina was my rock,' says Beverli. 'She helped me to walk out of the front door again and she was there whenever I needed her – a strong shoulder even though her world had crumbled too.'

In summer 2011, Beverli was still dealing with her PTSD when Tina suggested that they get her a puppy to keep her company while Tina was out at work, as an audiologist at a hospital.

'She hated leaving me in the morning because she didn't know what she was going to come back to,' says Beverli. 'Some days I would be happy and have a hot meal waiting; others she would come home to the house in darkness because I had closed all the curtains to shut the world out.

I was depressed, I know that now. I would stay in bed for hours and hours at a time, never eating, just lying there with my thoughts. There were times when I wanted to die because living was so terrifying for me.'

In the midst of despair came a crucial turning point in Beverli's life. Tina had seen an advert on a pet adoption website looking for people to take in a litter of Chinese Crested Hairless dogs who had been dumped in a woman's garden. Four had been adopted already but the rest needed good homes.

Beverli had already spotted a pup from this litter she thought she liked the look of. However, the woman whose garden the puppies had been dumped in and who was taking care of them in the meantime said that she was difficult and didn't warm to people as quickly as the others so, taking into account Beverli's fragile condition, perhaps she should consider a different dog.

It was a two-hour drive to see the dogs and Beverli tried not to get her hopes up. The moment she clapped eyes on the dog from the picture, though, she knew that this was 'the one'.

'She looked in my direction as soon as we went into the room and I bent down gently to say hello,' Beverli remembers. 'She had just had a bath and she smelt delicious. Her skin was so soft and she looked pretty – her eyes sparkled as she let me pet her. The little dog didn't seem nervous of me at all and, far from backing away and being unsociable, she let me pick her up. Her foster mum gave me a brush and I gently brushed through her thin fur as she sat motionless, staring at me all the time.'

'I can't believe this,' said her foster mum. 'You're the first person she has ever let pet her, let alone sit on their lap. I reckon she has chosen you to be her new mum.'

Beverli took her home that very day, naming her Piper. For almost the entire car ride home, Piper sat on her lap and looked up at her new owner as if she was checking that she was OK. Occasionally she would lick Beverli's nose gently or snuggle asleep as if the pair had known each other for years.

Piper and Beverli became constant companions. Wherever Beverli went, Piper would follow – even to the toilet! It was as if Piper wouldn't allow Beverli out of her sight for a second because the dog knew that she suffered when she was on her own. Even though she still hated to walk out of the front door into the world without Tina, Beverli started to walk Piper. At first, they only made it to the end of their driveway, but then they went down the street and soon they were walking to the park.

It was the knowledge that she had to make the effort for another soul that was the real turning point for Beverli.

'As a responsible person, I knew I had to get myself together to at least walk Piper twice a day, otherwise she would have been miserable,' says Beverli. 'Piper would fetch her leash and then come running to me – the signal that she was ready to go for a walk. I could never resist her huge, brown, faithful eyes, so I would pop my shoes and coat on, and we would venture out together. For the first time in years I didn't think about what might happen if I went out. I had to take care of my girl and that kind of took over my way of thinking. The

I could never resist her huge, brown, faithful eyes

first few times in the park were undeniably very frightening for me and once I almost had a panic attack. That time I felt as if my heart was going to burst out of my chest and I began to sweat, so Piper jumped up beside me on the park bench where I was sitting and she let me hold her until it passed. She made me feel safer just by being there.'

Piper seemed to have a sixth sense regarding when Beverli needed her. Sometimes when she woke up in the night after yet another horrifically vivid nightmare, Piper would be there to lick her tears and snuggle into bed with her. The days when Beverli closed the curtains and lay in darkness became fewer and further between because having Piper close by eased her black moods. Even on her darkest of days, when she felt sad and alone, Piper would pull the funniest of faces to make Beverli smile through her internal pain. There were times when Beverli couldn't help but burst into laughter whenever Piper was with her, and once she was able to laugh and smile, the dark thoughts miraculously went away. Piper was the perfect distraction and the best antidote for Beverli – far better, in fact, than all the pills she took every day just to get up in the morning.

Over a decade after the terrorist attack that could have killed her, Beverli has improved greatly. Her anxieties, her deep-rooted fears and her nightmares have been reduced. She can walk down the road with Piper and sirens no longer send her into panic mode. When she hears them, she picks Piper up and holds her close to her face until the noise has gone, then she carries on like nothing has happened.

Beverli can't even contemplate what might have happened if she hadn't found Piper. At the very least, she knows that she would still be housebound, unemployed, with an unfulfilled life.

The terrorist attacks would have destroyed her – and probably Tina too. Her new reality is far brighter, as Piper has helped her rebuild her life to such an extent that she believes in her future again.

'I truly believe that Piper chose me – I really didn't pick her,' says Beverli. 'When we met, she knew instinctively that I needed help, that I was a damaged soul in need of a miracle. She is that miracle, and I am so thankful that our paths crossed because she means the world to me. That dog has helped me in more ways than any pills or medicines ever could – she put me on the road to healing and I will be forever grateful to her for that. I may have given her a home but she repaid me more than I could have ever imagined. I am who I am today because of my precious Piper. She's a very special doggy.'

CHAPTER 2

LEE AND HERCULES'S STORY

Lee and his wife Elizabeth weren't exactly looking for a big dog of their own when they entered the Highland County Humane Society's dog shelter in Ohio. They had been helping their friend Tim look for his Jack Russell Terrier, Mimi, who had gone missing when he left his patio doors open. Tim was devastated that his tiny pooch had disappeared so when Lee and Elizabeth heard the news, they wanted to help. The thought of Mimi fending for herself in the countryside where they all lived was terrifying. There were coyotes and wolves in the woods who would have swallowed her right up, so they went from house to house in their neighbourhood looking for her.

When she didn't show up, the three of them split up and visited all the local animal shelters. There was still no sign of Mimi, so Lee and Elizabeth travelled into the next county just in case she had been taken to a shelter further away.

The Highland County dog shelter was full to capacity that day in November 2011. It was heartbreaking to see the dogs cooped up in the tiny pens, all needing homes. Most of them wagged their tails and ran to the front of their cages when the couple stopped by, but one resident caught their eye.

In the biggest cage of all was a St Bernard dog. He was about 45 kg – small for that breed – and his flanks and neck were covered in crusty, red sores. The St Bernard was obviously in some pain as he struggled to get up, but he still managed to greet Lee with a friendly bark and a lick on the hand through the cage's netting.

'What happened to him?' asked Lee.

'Hercules was found a few miles away in the middle of the woods by two hunters,' the shelter volunteer told him. 'He'd been attacked by coyotes and had multiple bite marks all over his body. The hunters couldn't leave him there as he was injured and so thin, so they carried him out of the woods and took him to a vet, where he was treated and then sent to us. The trouble is, he's really too big for us to take care of and he's been in here for too long. We need to get someone to take him on soon with his huge appetite and sizeable medical bills.'

As Lee and Elizabeth looked at Hercules, his bones sticking out all over the place and his sores bleeding, they knew that they couldn't let the handsome dog stay there a moment longer because it was clear he just needed a lot of love and more attention to put him on the road to recovery. Hercules was just two years old and despite all his wounds, he was a stunning looking dog who seemed to have a good attitude towards humans.

'The thought of him being put to sleep was just not an option,' recalls Lee. 'Here was a giant of a dog who was friendly and young, and we knew in our hearts he would make a great, loyal pet to someone. It wasn't fair that his only crime was being unwanted and that his punishment was death. Elizabeth and I looked at each other and there was no hesitation. We agreed to take him home right then and there. At the time we didn't think about how big he was and how he might take some serious training. We just wanted to get him to safety. We left the rescue centre that day not with Mimi but with our own dog, and we vowed to give him the kind of life he deserved. As big animal lovers we have had rescue dogs for years, so we knew what amazing, loving animals they can turn out to be. We were prepared to take the chance with Hercules and we didn't regret it.'

Hercules quickly established himself at his new home. He sniffed the whole place and finally settled down in the lounge, where he could keep an eye on his new owners.

At around 7 p.m., it was getting dark, so Lee let Hercules out of the back door that led to the back porch and into the garden so that he could go to the bathroom. As soon as he opened the door, Hercules started growling – and it definitely wasn't a friendly noise. It was a deep growl, as if he was trying to scare someone, and even though Lee told him to be quiet and calm down, the growling grew louder.

Hercules pulled himself away from Lee, who was holding his collar, and smashed straight through a screen door into the garden and bounded down the steps that led from the patio to the grass. This was where he started to chase a trespasser on Lee and Elizabeth's property. Hercules pursued the man to the fence and grabbed hold of his ankle to stop him from getting away, but the intruder freed himself and scrambled over the fence as Hercules barked like crazy and Lee looked on in astonishment.

When he was convinced the man had gone, Hercules limped back to Lee. Several of the wounds on his side had reopened during the hot pursuit. He was covered in blood so Lee gently ushered him into the house and called the police. While they waited for the police to arrive, the couple tended to their heroic dog's injuries. It felt surreal to them that he had only been living at their house for six hours and already had foiled a break-in.

The police turned up and searched the area, but the intruder was long gone. While they were investigating, they found that the house's phone line and TV cables had been cut and there were marks on the door where someone had been trying to break into their basement.

'I have no idea why our house was targeted like that because we honestly don't have anything much of value to take,' says Lee. 'It seemed that this was planned and the police said there was probably more than one burglar involved. I was more worried at the time about Hercules getting hurt. The poor boy stood so still so we could wash the sores that had opened up when he had leapt off the patio, over the staircase and into the garden. Hercules jumping up to get the burglar's ankle probably caused even more damage and I bet he gave the guy the fright of his life! He must have thought there was a monster chasing him in the dark! We took him

He had only been living at their house for six hours and already had foiled a break-in

to the vet and he was properly patched up. When we brought him home, we gave him a lovely big bone as a reward but it just didn't seem enough. Hercules didn't even really know us but he put his life on the line and he saved us from something much worse. What a hero!'

The local TV news stations heard about Hercules's valiant act and his story spread through the community like wildfire. Everyone loved the idea of the rescue dog who rescued his owners, and he subsequently received a Dog of Valor Award from The Humane Society of the United States.

As Hercules's story went viral, Mimi was found. A couple in the next county watched Lee on TV telling reporters how they came across Hercules when they were looking for another dog, and they recognised Mimi from his description. They had discovered her wandering the streets and when their numerous attempts to find her owners failed, they kindly took her in. When they saw the story, they realised they had Mimi and she was reunited with Tim. It was a wonderful ending to a story that has become legend in Ohio.

Hercules remains very protective of Lee and Elizabeth. If he feels that someone he doesn't know is too close to his owners, he stands in between them; if he's really unsure, he growls softly as a warning.

'There's no doubt he's a dog in a million,' says Lee proudly. 'From the time he moved in with us, he's taken care of us and he still walks the entire fence in the backyard every time he goes out there, as if he's making sure there's no one there. Some people might say that it was his lucky day when we found him because if we hadn't adopted him, he might not be alive today, but we always say it was ours because he definitely repaid the favour and rescued us. He's amazing.'

he's a dog in a million

CHAPTER 3

- -

SALLY AND BRIN'S STORY

The instant that Sally saw the photograph on the Internet of the thin, scruffy dog, she knew that she had to do something to help him. Brin had enormous brown, soulful eyes and, despite everything he had been through, looked like he had a good heart. The more she read about him, the more convinced she became that she had to act – before it was too late.

Brin was a street dog from Helmand, one of Afghanistan's most dangerous provinces, and he had a fascinating background.

He had apparently lived as a stray with a pack of other dogs until, in 2010, a group of British soldiers had found him barking furiously at something at the side of the road. One of the soldiers went to investigate and saw that he was barking at a hidden bomb device that would have blown up and killed the soldiers if they had stumbled upon it. They took the young dog in and cared for him, even though it was against army policy to have unofficial pets. Luckily for Brin, the captain of the base liked him and let him stay.

Brin possessed an uncanny gift for sniffing out bombs at roadsides or in the streets. Wherever the army would go, he would be at the front in his harness, leading the way. If Brin found something dangerous, he would bark to warn the soldiers. His keen snout and intuition for danger saved their lives many times over and they were extremely grateful.

During one bloody battle with the Taliban, British soldiers had to be airlifted to safety and, because they weren't allowed to take him in the army helicopter, Brin was reluctantly left behind to escape or die. Somehow the brave dog survived the gunfire and battle and found his way to a Taliban group. The Taliban thought he must be a valuable army dog, so they took him in, thinking he could be useful against the British forces.

Brin's British Army friends never forgot about him and when another battalion arrived in Helmand, they were told to keep their eyes open in case Brin returned to the area, looking for his old comrades. After some Afghan soldiers who were working with the Allied Forces found out Brin had been taken, he was rescued from the Taliban in a desperately sorry state. He was so thin his bones stuck out all over his body; he was riddled with fleas; and he had broken ribs and marks where he had been hit across his face. He had a huge, heavy chain around his neck, but when he was taken he still managed to wag his tail. The soldiers fed him and gently nursed him back to health.

Brin's story was so inspirational that it was featured on the Internet as one of the happier war stories. Sally could forget neither his handsome face nor his incredible survival story.

'Here was a dog who had survived one of the most dangerous war-torn areas in the world,' says Sally. 'He'd been rescued from the Taliban and I felt that he deserved a chance. He'd defied death so many times and he had helped our troops. I realised he couldn't stay in Afghanistan because it wasn't safe so I had this crazy idea to try to bring him to the UK to live out the rest of his days with one of the soldiers who had taken him in. I called the family of one of the soldiers who was featured in the article and I asked them if they thought it would be OK for me to help to bring Brin to the UK. They were all for it.'

Sally immediately set about fundraising. She called a dog charity close to where Brin was staying in Afghanistan and was told it would cost at least £4,000 to transport him to the UK. Undeterred, she called all the national newspapers in England to ask for publicity but received no response. No less determined, she contacted her local newspaper, in East Sussex, and managed to get a small piece in it. This was the start of a labour of love, a campaign that would take over her life – and she had the blessing of her husband Ray, a musician, and her sons George and Charlie, who thought it was a magnificent idea.

The newspaper article drummed up a lot of local support and inspired readers organised cake bakes and fundraisers. Sally put up dozens of posters asking for donations and help.

In three months, she had raised £5,000 and was able to pay for Brin to be flown to his new home, a place where there were no bombs, no fighting and the beautiful countryside to play in.

Sally had thought one of the soldiers would want to adopt him but they asked her to take him in instead. Although they loved the dog, Brin reminded them of the horrors of war that they had witnessed; they didn't feel strong enough mentally to keep him. Sally didn't hesitate with this change of plan, but she had no idea what she was letting herself in for. Brin was essentially a feral dog who didn't know what a leash was and who had scavenged for his own food before the army intervened.

Brin was smuggled onto a plane in Kabul, flown to Germany and then on to quarantine in Brighton. He set his paws on English soil on 16 September 2010 and Sally was there to meet him.

She had no idea how he was going to react to her as a woman. There was a male majority in the military and the Taliban and he was used to being around soldiers in Afghanistan. That first meeting, Sally lay down on her back in the cage and Brin sniffed her face gently. She put her hands on his chest and she lay there as still as could be while he sniffed her all over her body. He didn't once try to hurt her, as if he sensed that she was kind and she was going to take care of him.

While he was in quarantine he hardly barked and the staff thought he must be deaf due to the bombings he may have witnessed. It turned out that he wasn't deaf at all, but that he chose to be quiet if he couldn't see other dogs. This behaviour was a survival mechanism carried over from his roots in Afghanistan where, if he was quiet, he was safe to forage for food without other stray dogs attacking him.

Sally couldn't wait to get Brin home to meet her other pets, three rescue collies called Jake, Dennis and Ruby. When she did so, she started to realise quite how extraordinary this dog was.

The first day in his new home, he dug up her dead cat from the garden three times. As a stray, he was used to searching for his own food and sometimes killing for it. Sally cremated her cat rather than try reburying it.

Brin would often come into the house with pigeons or small rodents he had killed in the garden. He ran through a glass door while chasing a mouse because he had no concept that there was a barrier to stop him getting outside. He couldn't get used to being fed by a human or to having a bowl of water waiting for him whenever he felt thirsty. Often Sally would find him tearing up tree bark or plant stalks in his paws so that he could eat the middle of the stems for the moisture.

Brin hated rain so much that he would poop in the house because he refused to go out and get wet. Walks were another challenge because of his strength and because being on a leash wasn't natural for him. For the longest time he would bark if he heard a noise or if he saw anyone approaching them. If he saw another dog he would go insane and he was so powerful that Sally struggled to hold him. She quickly realised that he wasn't trying to attack anyone because barking was his defence mechanism, a warning to the other dogs that he was there. In Afghanistan, it was every dog for themselves so he had to be fierce for his self-preservation.

He was not a particularly affectionate dog for the first few months, preferring to sit close but not on top of Sally. Then one day, three months later, she washed his bed and lay on it to see if he would come to her willingly as she was on his 'territory'. She ended up falling asleep on it only to wake up to him snuggled right up against her body, as close as he could get. Sally burst into tears as she stroked his head and he didn't pull away like he often had before. It was a hugely emotional moment and a turning point for them both because it seemed to Sally that Brin finally felt safe enough in her company to let his guard down.

After that, he became very protective of Sally, even to the point that he didn't like her collies coming too close. Sally worked hard to show Brin that her other dogs were family members too and she didn't need protecting from them.

While Sally rescued Brin from a war zone, he has also helped her in countless ways. When she was in her twenties, she suffered blinding headaches and doctors couldn't determine what was wrong with her. When she was 34 years old, she suffered a stroke, fell into a coma and almost died. Doctors then diagnosed her with systemic lupus, a disease where her immune system mistakenly attacks healthy tissues in her body. This has had a huge impact on her life because a bad relapse can send her to bed for days in constant pain, or cause her to lose her speech for days on end and suffer horrendous fatigue.

The fundraising she carried out to get Brin to the UK was a miracle in itself because she was dealing with her lupus symptoms at the same time. There were occasions when she felt so ill she didn't know how she was going to get out of bed, yet the thought of saving this heroic dog fuelled her mind and her energy and somehow enabled her to manage her symptoms more effectively.

During her bedridden days, Brin will not leave Sally's side – he's her shadow. He curls up against Sally so tightly sometimes that it hurts her back but having him so close is therapeutic for her.

'It's the best feeling in the world to have him close by,' says Sally. 'As soon as we bonded, it was as if it became his job to care for me and just the feel of his body next to mine and his warm breath on my neck allows me to relax and get my energy back. If I'm having a bad day and I'm feeling down and sorry for myself, I just look at him. Brin has been through so much that we'll never know half the atrocities he witnessed, or the cruelty he faced at the hands of the Taliban, yet he's still here, so engaging, always wagging his tail, making the most of every day. I find his attitude inspirational and he cheers me up no end just by being there in the same room as me. I often get up just because I know that he needs to go out or that he needs me to feed him or give him a loving pat. I can't let the lupus get me down because he relies on me more than any dog I've ever known and I won't let him down.'

As his story has been shared by so many people, Sally has been asked to give community talks and host more fundraisers to help other army dogs come to start a new life in the UK.

'Without him, I would never have had the confidence and I know I would've used the lupus as an excuse not to go out and do it. The lupus controlled my social life for many years, to the point where I didn't have one. With Brin's notoriety, I've made so many new friends and we get invited out all of the time to functions and dinners. I feel like he's given me a new lease of life and I'll be forever grateful to him for that.'

Brin was also there for Sally when her older brother, Ellis, from whom she had been estranged for several years, committed suicide in January 2014. He had become increasingly reliant on their mother, and when she grew older and incapacitated, he couldn't take it; Ellis killed himself rather than live without her.

'It was a desperately sad time for me,' says Sally. 'While it wasn't a shock because I'd always felt that he would do something like that, it was still hard to hear. My brother had been an alcoholic all his life, and I think his life just became too difficult. Although I didn't have any regrets, there was nothing I could have done, I was still sad that my brother was gone. Brin and I would go for walks in the forest and I would sit in my thinking spot and just cry and cry with Brin next to me. He was such a comfort, as if he knew what I was going through. Just knowing he was there to lick away my tears and never leave me alone was such a big thing for me. He's a very intuitive animal to my feelings and he knows when I'm sad, happy, anxious or just plain angry about something. Brin has helped me through some of the worst times of my life and if it hadn't been for his love and support, I'm not sure I'd be the person I am today.'

Sally has since adopted a stray from the Ukraine called Trinny, a street dog who would turn up at the army base every day with a pack of other dogs, looking for food. One day she didn't show up so the soldiers looked for her and found her dying in the street, two legs broken so badly that the bone was poking out of one of them. The soldier patched her up and she was treated for blood poisoning from her wounds – the septicaemia almost killed her.

Sally paid for Trinny to be brought to England and now she and Brin are the best of friends, probably because their backgrounds are so similar that they understand each other.

'My Trinny girl is an absolute joy too,' says Sally. 'She was in a horrible state when she was found but since she's been living here, she's thrived. Brin can't get enough of her and when he's not with me, he's playing with her. She's also very protective and affectionate towards me and she's a great friend to me too. I'm still fundraising to bring other dogs home from the war. They inspire me every day to get up and to be a better person. If I'm feeling depressed with my lupus, I only have to look at them both and I genuinely feel better. They're the best medicine anyone could ever have.'

CHAPTER 4

- -

HEIDI AND CHILLY'S STORY

It was Chilly's lucky day when Heidi walked into the Fluvanna animal shelter in Virginia to find a suitable Bull Terrier for her friend to adopt. Heidi, who has fostered unwanted dogs for most of her adult life, wasn't looking for another pet of her own, but the pretty English Pit Bull mix dog caught her eye.

She was a larger breed, brown and white dog, with a cuddly face and the brightest of eyes. As soon as Chilly saw Heidi through the bars of her cage, she ambled over to say a friendly hello.

There was an instant connection between the two. Heidi quickly decided that she had to take Chilly home with her, even though she already had four other smaller breed dogs.

Chilly was around three or four years old and had been in the shelter for five weeks, after someone found her wandering the streets and took her to the shelter. She had a name tag and a phone number around her collar but her original owner didn't want her back, so she was put up for adoption.

'I still don't understand why her owner didn't come to collect her,' says Heidi. 'From the moment I met her, she was the gentlest of animals, very quiet but also as friendly as a dog can be. There wasn't a bad bone in her body and I just had to take her home with me. At the time I was fostering a mum and nine puppies and I also had four much smaller dogs of my own, so a part of me was worried about whether they would mix OK. It was a lot of animals under one roof! I needn't have worried at all. Everyone loved her and she made special friends with Madeline, a small Dachshund mix who had chemical burns. I was fostering the poor girl, who had sores all over her body, and Chilly paid extra attention to her as if she knew she had been hurt. She would play tug of war with Madeline and sleep next to her at night like she was caring for her. That told me a lot about the type of dog Chilly was and I fell even more in love.'

Three months after Chilly's adoption, it was the animal's turn to show Heidi how much she loved her – and she did so in spectacular fashion.

On 7 September 2012, Heidi, who is highly allergic to pollen, mould, mildew and grasses, was at her doctor's office waiting for allergy shots. Her allergies had triggered several serious asthma attacks during recent months and her doctor had advised her to get the shots to relieve her symptoms and prevent further breathing problems.

The nurse gave Heidi one injection in each arm but within a few minutes her hands started to sweat and her face turned bright red. Her ears felt like they were on fire and her throat started to hurt as if there were sharp needles poking her.

It turned out that the nurse had mistakenly given her 14 times the correct dose and Heidi was going into anaphylactic shock as a reaction to all the medicine in her bloodstream. Thankfully she was still in her doctor's office when she fell ill and they recognised the potentially life-threatening condition, so they were able to treat her with EpiPens and other medicines.

The huge doses of Benadryl to counteract the allergy shots caused Heidi to feel so ill and sleepy that she couldn't possibly drive her car, so her dad Robert came to pick her up and take her back home.

When she got home, she lay on the sofa with a blanket while her dad put the dogs outside so that they didn't get in the way while she was resting. Chilly would not leave her side and protested loudly when Robert tried to move her, so he left her with Heidi in the living room.

About thirty minutes after Robert had left his daughter to sleep, Chilly tried to wake her up and get her off the sofa. She pounded on Heidi's chest with her giant paws and attempted to pull her big hair bow out with her teeth. Heidi tried to wake up when she felt Chilly on her chest but she could barely open her eyes. It was only when she tried to speak to her dog that she realised her throat was closing up and that she was struggling to breathe.

She was in full-blown anaphylactic shock and her dog was desperately trying to save her life!

'Chilly never jumps up on my lap unless I tell her that she can and she certainly doesn't ever paw me like she did that day,' says Heidi. 'She knew that I was in serious trouble and she wasn't going to stop until she woke me up. I've never been so terrified. I could barely swallow and I couldn't shout for help. My heart was racing like crazy as I tried to get some air in my lungs and breathe, but it was no use. I was also still feeling drowsy from the Benadryl and that's why she kept hammering me in my chest – she was keeping me awake. I know that if I'd gone back to sleep, I would have died. I would've gone to sleep and never woken up again, but Chilly wasn't going to let that happen. It was her persistence that kept me alive.'

Heidi had her phone next to her so she dialled 911. She had to press the automated response buttons to ask for help because she couldn't speak. Thankfully, the paramedics arrived within a few minutes. Her daughter Caitlyn arrived home from the school bus at the same moment.

Horrified, Caitlyn and her boyfriend, who was stopping by for dinner, followed the ambulance to the University of Virginia Hospital. During the ride, Heidi stopped breathing and had to be resuscitated.

'I had blacked out but I could still hear every word,' recalls Heidi. 'I heard the lady paramedic shouting, "We're

It was her persistence that kept me alive

losing her, we're losing her." Then I heard her call someone to ask if she could give me medicine to open my throat so that I could breathe. I was in a shocking way when I arrived at the hospital. I had angry red blotches all over my body and it looked like I'd been scalded by boiling hot water. I was given another two EpiPens and more medication during my two-day hospital stay. My doctors said I was extremely lucky that Chilly had been there to wake me up. My dog saved my life and I'll never be able to thank her enough for what she did that day.'

The story of how Chilly the rescue dog rescued her owner from death quickly made the local and national news. The pair appeared in newspapers and on TV as the story caught the public's imagination. Chilly's heroics even beat off stiff competition to win a national Pet of Valor award, given by The Humane Society of the United States in 2013.

From that fateful day onwards, Chilly has been extra protective of Heidi, who has since been diagnosed with sleep apnoea, which means she has one or two pauses in her breathing during sleep. Chilly is acutely aware of her condition, and she jumps on Heidi's chest and licks her face to wake her up and kick-start her breathing again. It's even more incredible that Chilly has this sixth sense when you stop to think that the dog has received no formal training to detect or treat human illnesses.

The dog that nobody wanted has proved time and time again that she is worth her weight in gold.

I'll never be able to thank her enough for what she did that day

'Chilly always knows when something is wrong,' says Heidi. 'Sometimes my daughter says that I love my dog more than I love her because we do have a special bond! She has had a huge impact on my life. I'll be crushed when her time comes because she has become not just my guardian angel but my second child and protector, confidante and all-round sidekick. She isn't trained as a medical dog – she just loves me for me!'

CHAPTER 5

JOSIE AND TED'S STORY

Josie and her husband Brian had always owned rescue dogs and they particularly loved the Border Collie breed, so when Josie decided that she wanted another pet after their beloved dog died, the couple looked everywhere for a suitable match. Josie had a particular reason for getting another dog: to provide company for her teenage daughter Megs. She had always been an introverted girl who had few friends and who preferred her own company. Josie thought a new pup would give her something to focus on and perhaps it would bring her out of her shell.

During their search to find a Border Collie to adopt, they came across an advert on the Gumtree listings website where a man was advertising for a new home for his dog. From his cute profile, Josie and Megs thought this could be 'the one', so Brian arranged to call in to see the 15-month-old pup on the way from a wedding in Plymouth back to their home in the north-east of England.

When they arrived and banged on the owner's front door, it was only a few seconds before the man raced out of the house with the dog wriggling in his arms. He shoved the animal straight into the car before Josie could ask any questions about the pup's background. Ignoring the couple, he went back into the house and refused to open the door again. It was a bizarre situation and, even if they didn't want the collie, they couldn't leave him because it was obvious his owner wanted nothing whatsoever to do with him.

'The dog was shaking and literally crying on the back seat of our car,' recalls Josie. 'He wasn't a huge dog and he had the most mournful eyes I've ever seen. They were so sad and they were tearing up as I gently stroked his soft head. As I examined him, it was clear that there was something wrong with his back legs. They looked a bit crooked and a lot smaller than the rest of his body. His fur was overgrown and matted and it looked like he had fleas. There was no way we were going to leave him because it was clear that he'd been mistreated. I didn't like the fact that the man had stooped as low as to dump him on us but, on the other hand, I wasn't going to ask him to take him back or dump the dog at a rescue shelter. I had to take him home.'

The next day, Josie took Ted, the newly named dog, to her vet to be examined. The vet's findings almost broke her heart. Ted's back legs looked deformed because his muscles had wasted away, probably because he hadn't been exercised enough. He walked with a lopsided gait because, the vet concluded, he had been cooped up in a cage that was far too small for his size and he hadn't been able to move around freely. The dog was also very sensitive to light, suggesting that he had lived most of his young life in a tiny cage that was covered with something, perhaps a blanket, for most of the time. It appeared that Ted hadn't been out in daylight or seen bright lights before.

Additionally, Ted seemed confused when Josie spoke to him or if she gave a command. Border Collies are known to be one of the dog kingdom's most intelligent creatures, but sometimes he just didn't seem to understand what she was saying to him. His head often felt hot and he would cry, as if he was suffering from a bad headache. All this meant that Josie took him back and forth between their house and the vet in the first few days. The vet thought Ted was displaying symptoms of being kicked hard in the head when he was a puppy.

Josie could not believe that someone could be so cruel to an animal. Her instinct was to shower the poor boy with as much love and affection as he could handle. The thought of his abuse made her furious but also incredibly sad and she was determined to show him what a caring, loving family could do to make him feel happy and safe.

During the first few weeks, it was obvious Ted was scared of people. Josie bought him the biggest cage she could find and she set it up in the lounge with a blanket draped over the top. It was large enough

He had lived most of his young life in a tiny cage

for him to move around in easily so he would not feel trapped. Brian took the door off the cage so Ted could go in and out as he pleased. He would often lie in there contentedly because it was all he had ever known. Gradually, he ventured out but it was a long eight months before he completely stopped using the cage as his safe zone.

Ted just needed the time and the space to settle down and to learn to trust his new family. He would frequently pee on the floor because something unnerved him or if he was left alone. The poor dog had so much anxiety to cope with that sometimes Josie wondered if he would ever just be a regular dog – and, as it turns out, he's anything but.

Josie suffers from ME, the chronic fatigue syndrome that causes severe exhaustion and sickness. For the past 25 years she has battled the debilitating condition but it has left her housebound much of the time. She experiences good days – when she feels well enough to go out and meet friends or go for a walk or a shopping trip – but those days are few and far between. For the most part, she is bedridden, sleeping, or she camps out on her sofa.

While it became clear that Ted loved the whole family in his own way, it was Josie who he really connected with. He slept in bed with her all day, close to her face so she knew he was there. When she got up he would follow at her side, sometimes pushing himself against her legs if she stumbled into the wall or down the hall because her legs were so tired. Although Josie is accustomed to being bedridden with little energy, it's still hugely frustrating and lonely to be unable to do everything she wants to with her family. Sometimes she just needed to have a cry at the unfairness of the situation, and having Ted's loyal companionship helped her moods.

In December 2014, Josie noticed a small, hard lump in her left breast. She has a history of benign lumps in both breasts, and because this one was painful she thought it couldn't be cancerous because she'd read that malignant lumps don't hurt when you touch them.

Two days later, she was watching TV with Ted and Brian on the sofa in the living room, when Ted abruptly jumped off his bed and onto Josie's lap. He shoved his cold nose into her left armpit and onto her left breast, making the oddest noise, like he was wailing and in distress.

'I had never heard anything like it,' Josie recounts. 'It was like he was screaming to get my attention because whatever it was mattered – it was urgent. For a dog who barely barked or made a noise, I knew there was something going on. He then knocked me backwards on the sofa and he started to pummel my left boob with his front paws. There was no doubt in my mind that he was trying to alert me to the lump on my breast because he was hurting me. I'd read in the newspapers about dogs detecting cancer before their owners even know they're ill, and I believe that they can do that because their sense of smell and instinct are so highly developed. Ted was so upset that day that I told Brian I was going to the doctor to get the lump checked out. It turned out to be the best thing I could have done.'

The very next day, Josie went to see her doctor, who told her that he thought it was a cancerous lump. Due to the urgency of her situation, she was seen within a couple of days by specialists at her local hospital, where a biopsy and blood tests confirmed that she was seriously ill. Josie was suffering from one of the deadliest types of cancer.

She underwent a lumpectomy to remove the tumour. Luckily, because it was detected so quickly, it hadn't spread to other parts of her body. The surgeons told her that it was such an aggressive, fast-spreading tumour that if she hadn't sought medical help when she did, she would have been dead by the following March.

As a precaution to ensure that there were no rogue cancer cells in her body, Josie was given 18 weeks of chemotherapy followed by 25 sessions of radiation therapy, which very nearly killed her because her ME weakened her ability to recover.

It was a testing time for the whole family, Ted included. When Josie was in hospital, he fretted and wouldn't rest or eat. A local dog walker took him out for free when she heard about Josie's situation but it was obvious he didn't want to be out without his mum. He would pull on his leash to get home when he was out with the dog walker. There was no doubt in Brian's mind that Ted didn't want to leave the house in case Josie returned home and he wasn't there to greet her.

As soon as she came home, Ted practically glued himself to her side. He was there when she was feeling sick to her stomach with the chemotherapy, when she was nursing painful burns on her body from the radiation therapy, and when she just needed a good cry because she was overwhelmed.

'With Ted, I could be myself,' says Josie. 'I was always reassuring Brian and Megs and my friends that I was doing well, that I was going to beat the cancer and that everything was going to turn out right. I had to be strong for them because they were so frightened they might lose me.

'But it was hard being so upbeat all the time. I didn't know for sure I was going to get well and there were days when I honestly thought I was dying. The signs were good that the cancer was gone but anything could have happened – you just never know when you're suffering from such a horrible disease. I used to cry, holding Ted in my bed. I'd tell him how I felt at that moment and he would lick my nose gently as if to say he understood and he was there for me. He would curl up and somehow wrap his legs around mine to make me feel safe. Ted was probably my best comfort because I didn't have to pretend and being able to let my guard down once in a while and have a good cry was good for me. I'd get all the negative thoughts out of my head and feel stronger and more optimistic thanks to Ted.'

Ted's story doesn't stop there either. Megs suffers from Type 1 diabetes and has to inject herself with insulin daily. Ted has been known on many occasions to alert Josie that Megs's blood sugar is too low or too high. If he's in Megs's bedroom while she's studying and he detects that her levels aren't right, he will find Josie and Brian and herd them towards Megs so that they administer life-saving medicine or food to settle her system. He will cock his head to one side like he's telling them, 'Come on, hurry up!'

The first time it happened, Megs was in bed asleep and Ted was frantic when he came looking for Josie. He was barking and running circles around her to get her attention, so she followed him up the stairs to Megs's room.

When she tested her blood sugar levels, they were critically low and she was in danger of lapsing into a diabetic coma. Thankfully, because of Ted, Josie woke her up and gave her an insulin injection that may have saved her life.

'Beyond a shadow of a doubt Ted saved my life,' says Josie. 'Somehow he detected that I had cancer. I still can't believe it sometimes but it's all true. I'd be dead and buried if it wasn't for my beautiful Ted. Considering his background we're incredibly lucky that he's such an amazing dog. He has the biggest heart and I know how much he loves his family. Ted is such a huge part of our family – he saved Megs too and I will be forever grateful to him for always being alert for both me and Megs. I thank God every day that he came into our home.'

CHAPTER 6

DEBBIE AND TOBY'S STORY

Ever since she was a little girl, Debbie has had a profound love for animals of all kinds, particularly dogs. She dreamed of a house full of pets so it was natural that when she married her husband Kevin, they decided to get dogs when the time was right.

Instead of buying their new family member from a breeder, Debbie decided to adopt an unwanted pooch from a local charity near their home in North East, Maryland, in order to give it a kind, loving home. Their pet search ended with Fred, a sweet, four-year-old Basset Hound, who had experienced the worst life imaginable.

He had been used as a bait dog by a ring of illegal Pit Bull dog fighters. When he was finally rescued from a certain death and was ready to be rehomed, he was still in very poor shape.

Although slowly healing, his emaciated body was covered with deep bite marks and scratches. There were so many scars from previous maulings that it was obvious he had been used extensively as a bait dog. It was a miracle he was even alive.

Debbie brought him home straight away, but it took Fred a long time to trust her and Kevin and to realise that he was safe in their house. Poor Fred had severe emotional issues and particularly hated loud noises. There was a high school at the back of their house and when the school band practised, Fred would tremble and cry so much that he would have to be sedated. During thunderstorms, even when he was with Debbie, his terror was such that he would hyperventilate and pass out. It was an awful shame that he had been reduced to this state, but with a lot of love, care and attention, he slowly settled down and started to love again.

Fred took up a lot of their time, so Debbie wasn't planning on adopting another dog for a while. Out of the blue, she received a phone call from a friend while she was visiting her dad Sam at his home in Delaware. Sam has Alzheimer's and Debbie split her time between her home in Maryland and her dad's house so that she could care for him. This friend was a fellow dog lover who needed Debbie's help.

'Could you foster a puppy?' the friend asked. 'We've had word of a family of pups who have been abandoned who need taking care of. Can you come out now?'

There was no way Debbie could turn down a plea for help, so she drove out to the back of the local shopping centre, where the five puppies had been found in a dirty old skip. Someone had dumped them there and they were at death's door. The poor babies were a sorry sight. All of them were very tiny, their eyes still closed, squeaking out for help as they struggled to move over the mounds of rotting rubbish. When Debbie took hold of one of the puppies, she knew immediately that she had to take care of this little mite and that she wasn't just going to foster him – she was going to adopt him as a friend for Fred.

'It was heartbreaking,' recalls Debbie. 'The little dog was filthy and he smelled to high heaven. His tiny eyes were closed shut because of the garbage all around them and he had an infection.

He was riddled with fleas and maggots, so goodness knows how long they had been in there. When you see such cruelty, it really does question your faith in human nature. I couldn't understand how anyone could have left these defenceless animals on their own to die. As soon as I had one of the pups in my hands, I knew that I wasn't going to be able to give him up. I couldn't trust anyone else to love and care for him the way I knew I could, and after such an awful start to his life I felt that he deserved the best.'

Debbie gave the pup, a pure white Golden Retriever, a warm bath then she took him to the vet. She was warned that given his serious condition, he might not make it, so she should prepare herself for the worst.

The days were long caring for the sick puppy. He had to be bottle-fed every few hours and needed large amounts of medication to get rid of the maggots and the numerous infections that plagued his small body.

After a week, Debbie started to see an improvement. Soon after that first week, the puppy she named Toby came on literally in leaps and bounds as he found his strength and discovered how much fun life with Debbie, Kevin and Fred was.

It took about two months to nurse Toby to good health. Debbie kept in contact with the people who fostered the other puppies and was devastated to learn of their deaths – Toby was the sole survivor. During his recovery time, Toby bonded well with the couple but particularly with Debbie. It was as if he knew that she had saved his life and he wanted to be near her all the time. He would follow her all over the house and never leave her side.

She took him to dog-training classes and he loved their time together, barking with glee when she told him to get in the car so that they could drive to obedience school. Toby made a bit of a dog's dinner of his obedience classes, though. He was growing into a handsome dog who was full of energy and who didn't want to learn anything – he wanted to play all the time. Toby was hilarious – he would sit when he was supposed to stand up straight. He would walk left instead of right, or would back up instead of walking forward on his lead.

Debbie struggled to keep her patience sometimes – and Toby could be embarrassing when he flat-out refused to obey her commands – but he kept her entertained and did eventually pass obedience school!

Despite his naughty behaviour, Debbie knew that Toby loved and appreciated her. As it turned out, when he was two years old, Toby had the chance to show her just how much she meant to him.

A year after Toby entered her world, Debbie decided to set up a jewellery-designing business from home so that Fred and Toby wouldn't be at the house all day long. She would take them out three or four times a day and Toby was perfect company when she was working at home. He loved to gambol around the garden playing with his toys, then he would laze at Debbie's feet in her office, snoozing peacefully and waiting for treats. Sometimes when Debbie took a break from work, they would lie in the sunshine together while she tickled his soft, furry head. They had such a close bond and she would have done anything for him.

It was a quiet afternoon in 2007 at Debbie's house. On this ordinary day, she decided to have an apple after lunch. Usually she peeled apples because she hated the skin but she had just read a magazine article saying that the skin is the best part of the fruit, so she decided to eat it to be healthier.

Suddenly, a piece of apple got stuck in her throat. She tried to cough it out but it wouldn't budge. She banged her chest hard to see if that would help. It didn't.

Debbie's heart started to pound as she realised that she was choking. The piece of apple was stuck so fast that she couldn't catch her breath and she was gasping for air.

She ran into the kitchen and threw herself on the back of a chair because she remembered an old schoolteacher showing her class the Heimlich manoeuvre, a proven way of dislodging the item from someone who is choking.

She tried this procedure three times, but nothing happened and she started to really panic.

'I honestly thought I might die,' recalls Debbie. 'In my mind's eye I imagined Kevin walking into the house and finding me dead on the floor with a half-eaten apple next to my cold body.

Debbie's heart started to pound as she realised that she was choking

But I couldn't think what to do next. I couldn't get into the street and shout for help and I couldn't dislodge it myself. Everything started to go black, and the more I gasped for air, the more I choked. It was the most terrifying moment of my life. I didn't think I would see my husband or my beloved animals again. I was going to die alone, an agonising death.'

Except that Debbie wasn't alone. As she staggered towards the hallway, Toby appeared out of nowhere, running at full pelt, and he knocked her onto her back. If she hadn't been choking, she would have had the wind knocked out of her lungs.

Toby never jumped at people, so this was new. Although he was boisterous and liked to play, in all the time she'd owned him, he had never jumped to greet anybody. Yet now he knocked Debbie over so violently and with such urgency, she didn't even have time to wonder why.

As she lay there, stunned, Toby pummelled her chest twice with his big, muddy paws. With 40 kg of dog pounding her chest, the pain was excruciating.

But then… whoosh! The apple flew out of Debbie's mouth, and she became aware of Toby's big brown eyes staring at her as she opened her eyes. She wasn't choking any more, and tears of relief fell down her cheeks.

Debbie slowly pulled herself up and leaned against the kitchen wall. Toby licked her face gently as she tried to catch her breath. She wrapped her arms around her hero as she realised that he had truly saved her life.

'I don't know if it was divine intervention or the angels helping but Toby saved my life that day,' says Debbie. 'I think he saw that my Heimlich manoeuvre didn't work so he instinctively tried his own doggy version of it. I remember that everything was going black because I was passing out when he knocked me backwards and pummelled my chest. I don't think he would have stopped until that apple had come out. Lucky for me, he hit me in just the right places. We sat there for ages in the kitchen as I caught my breath. He wouldn't take his eyes off me and he just showered me with kisses until I finally managed to get up and stagger to the sofa.'

Not long after, the front door opened and a client who was booked for a design lesson from Debbie walked into the house. Shocked to see Debbie lying on the sofa and to hear her incredible story, she rushed her to the hospital for a check-up.

The doctor found bruises around Debbie's ribcage and a big red paw print on her heart – proof that her beloved boy had saved her life. It was an emotional time for Debbie, who has never eaten apple peel since.

The local newspaper heard about Toby's heroics and soon he became a national hero. Debbie, Toby and Fred travelled to New York in November 2007, when Toby was named the American Society for the Prevention of Cruelty to Animals (ASPCA) Dog of the Year.

A few months after Toby's honour, he started to limp and was diagnosed with stage four bone cancer in his front right leg. He was just three years old, and Debbie and Kevin were devastated to hear the grim diagnosis.

'Toby had been limping a little bit for a while,' says Debbie. 'One of his front legs was a little deformed from birth, so we thought it must just be arthritis, so the cancer diagnosis was a massive shock. I remember taking the call and when I heard the news, I collapsed on the floor, hysterically crying. I don't know who cried more, me or my husband, but we were beyond devastated for our beautiful boy. It seemed so unfair that after his cruel start in life, this could have happened to him. It was even worse because he had saved my life and I couldn't fathom out why, after being such a hero, he was rewarded with what could have been a death sentence.'

After they had dried their tears, Debbie and Kevin decided to find a vet who specialised in canine cancer treatment.

They found a local specialist and a personalised treatment plan was devised for Toby. Sadly, it involved amputating his front right leg. This didn't make the slightest bit of difference to Toby, though, as it didn't stop him bounding around on three legs, full of energy and enthusiasm.

After his leg was taken, Toby had radiation therapy then chemotherapy for several weeks. His owners were absolutely thrilled when he was declared to be in remission.

However, the respite was brief as the cancer returned mere months later. This time, Toby was given more intensive chemotherapy. Just as with humans, the chemotherapy made him sick sometimes, although special medication helped, and some of his fur fell out. He went into remission again, and Toby is still cancer-free at ten years old.

Debbie has opened a store in Maryland called Toby the Golden Hero Gifts, where she sells gifts and jewellery to raise money to help pay the expensive veterinarian bills of other owners whose dogs have cancer.

Toby goes to the store with Debbie every day and he's still quite the celebrity. Children and adults from all over stop by to pay him a visit. It seems that it's particularly children with disabilities who find comfort in being around Toby.

'I opened the store as a way to give back to the world as thanks that Toby survived cancer,' says Debbie. 'It's a miracle he's still with us and I wanted to help other people facing similar life-changing challenges. I am so proud of

he's a beacon of hope to the
people who visit him

Toby. We've had kids in here with only one leg who love to play with him because he shows them that life doesn't have to end if you're physically challenged or different from others. He's my angel in fur. I can still remember how tiny he was when we rescued him and I know that he was always grateful to us for giving him a loving, safe home. Somehow he's always known that we helped him when he was a pup in need. He was the only one of his brothers and sisters who survived that skip and I think that God had a plan for him. Not only did he save my life, but he's a beacon of hope to the people who visit him. Toby may be getting old and he's riddled with arthritis, but when he sees a little girl who wants to play, he's always got the time for some fun. I can honestly say that my rescue dog really did rescue me and I will be forever in his debt. He's unique, that's for sure, and now it's my turn to take care of him. I swear that when I look into Toby's eyes I see the kindest hearted soul and I'm just so lucky that he's mine.'

CHAPTER 7

CHRISTIAN AND OBI'S STORY

Sarah and Jason's son Christian had always been what they called 'quirky'. He didn't have many friends because he found it difficult to make them – let alone keep them. He didn't mix well with the other children at school, preferring to be by himself in the playground, away from the hustle and bustle. He didn't have any of the more usual interests of a boy his age; instead he had a fixation with robots and making things.

Sarah and Jason had taken their son to countless doctors in Northamptonshire where they live because they knew instinctively that something wasn't quite right with Christian, but they were consistently told that he was fine and that they should simply let him be himself. Yet Sarah had a niggling feeling that Christian was so different to other boys his age that she was convinced something was going on in his young head – she just couldn't put her finger on what it was, despite trawling the Internet looking for clues.

Things grew far worse in June 2009, when Sarah's father was in a hospice dying from cancer. Christian was very close to his grandfather, insisting that he wanted to see him every day.

Even though a hospice isn't necessarily an ideal place for children, Sarah didn't argue. Besides, her father loved seeing his grandson and Christian was helping to make his last days on earth as happy as possible. Christian became obsessed with being at the hospice with his grandfather. If Sarah said he couldn't go then he would have a screaming fit, and she would relent to avoid a further scene.

A poster on a wall in the hospice advertised the importance of handwashing and hand-sanitising for those visiting the residents; germs in a hospice could prove fatal. Christian took this advice to heart and began to frantically wash his hands all the time, particularly when visiting his grandfather. He wouldn't go into his grandfather's room unless he had scrubbed his hands, then he would scrub his hands again when he left the hospital. At the same time, Christian stopped eating because he said he felt sick.

'Looking back, I believe that the handwashing was the only control that Christian felt he had to help his grandfather,' recalls Sarah. 'He would wash his hands several times a day until he couldn't stop. He couldn't stop his grandfather from dying, but he could control being safe around him by not bringing germs into his room. He made us all do the same and if we didn't, he would know and have a go at us. Then he said he felt like he was going to throw up all the time, so he stopped eating, which made matters worse. When his grandfather eventually passed away, he started having terrible meltdowns. Christian couldn't control himself when he was in the middle of a rage and, honestly, it was frightening to see him because there was little we could to stop or help him. It was as if he were in a world of his own.'

Christian's obsessions became more intense as he struggled to come to terms with his grandfather's passing. He would wash and scrub his hands so vigorously that the skin rubbed off and they bled. Then he would clean them some more.

He developed a fear of germs, becoming convinced that things like aerosol cans could contaminate, harm and make him ill. His family was forced to get rid of all sprays, such as air fresheners and deodorants, because he couldn't be around them.

At her wits' end, Sarah took her son to see his doctor again. Finally, aged 11, Christian was referred to the Child and Adolescent Mental Health Services, a government health body. Specialist mental health doctors diagnosed him with autism and obsessive–compulsive disorder. This was a huge relief for his parents – to be given a name for his condition felt like half the battle. In retrospect, Christian had displayed classic symptoms of autism for years but, because they weren't severe, it had been overlooked by his paediatrician. At least now his parents knew what they were up against and could learn how to cope with it.

It was during an autism conference that Sarah met the group Dogs for the Disabled. Their workshop on how dogs could help support a person with disabilities showed Sarah and other parents with autistic children just how much a service dog could help their children lead more normal lives. Studies had demonstrated that autistic children with dogs were better equipped to manage their symptoms because pets somehow made them feel safer, calmer and happier.

This was something that had never occurred to Sarah before – ironically, because Christian owned a dog already.

When Christian was seven years old, the family adopted a cute little, brown-and-tan Jack Russell puppy from a lady whose dog had had puppies and who was finding good homes for all of them. Obi was the runt of the litter. No one seemed to want him because he was tiny, a weak bag of bones who struggled to feed. No one except Christian, that is, who wanted Obi as soon as he saw him and took him home there and then.

During Christian's meltdowns, Sarah had got into the habit of shutting Obi in a room until her son calmed down, for fear that he might turn physical and that Obi might get caught in the crossfire. Dealing with Christian was difficult at the best of times, but when he was having a tantrum, he was like a different, stronger person – someone Sarah didn't recognise.

After the workshop, Sarah started to see Obi differently. What if keeping her son and his dog apart was doing more harm than good? What if Obi could help Christian cope with his mood swings and meltdowns? Sarah wondered if, by trying to do the right thing, she had unknowingly separated Christian from the one being that could help him.

Instead of locking Obi away, Sarah experimented and watched to see what effect the little dog had on her son. She immediately became aware that Obi rarely left Christian's side. If Christian was distressed and upset, Obi would follow him and make a beeline for his lap, and her son's terrible mood would dissipate just as quickly as he had fallen into a temper.

It seemed that just to have Obi by his side, licking his hand or letting him pet his soft, furry head, was enough to calm Christian down and to set him thinking straight again. The thought of him hurting his little dog in some way made him stop screaming a lot quicker than his mum ever could.

Christian found it difficult to sleep properly, waking up at all hours of the night and being unable to go back to sleep. In turn, Sarah experienced endless sleepless nights as she didn't trust Christian to be awake and on his own. Needless to say, it was exhausting for her.

One night, Sarah let Obi sleep with Christian in bed, snuggled on the pillow next to his. For the first time in years, he slept most of the night, and it was amazing the difference a good night's sleep made to Christian's outlook. He was not only calmer but happier too.

During bad periods, Christian experienced meltdowns up to 15 times a day but their regularity decreased significantly the more Obi was around him. Instead of Christian pacing the room, flapping his hands in a rage and screaming at the top of his voice, he sat on the bed and spoke quietly to Obi. Instead of pushing furniture around because he was frustrated with something or someone, Christian learned to keep control because he didn't want Obi to see him in such a foul mood. He felt the need to protect his little dog and that, in turn, forced him to take a deep breath and relax.

'I saw such a huge difference in my son almost as soon as I let Obi spend more time with Christian. It was like magic,' says Sarah. 'I couldn't believe that I hadn't thought that Obi could help him before. I suppose I'd always been worried that Christian might have hurt his dog during a tantrum, or that Obi would have got in the way while we were dealing with what was happening with Christian. The reality was that Obi was such a calming influence on Christian and if it hadn't been for the Dogs for the Disabled, we would never have known. It was like a light had been switched on in his brain and the bad times were far fewer.'

Obi likes routine, so Christian has a reason to get up early each morning to walk his best friend. Even when he feels like staying in bed, Christian is aware of his responsibility so he drags himself out and feels all the better for it.

Christian was always shy but having Obi has truly brought him out of his shell. He has met other people on his dog walks who ask him about Obi, and this interest in his dog diverts the attention away from himself, which makes Christian feel more settled and confident.

He used to have severe panic attacks during which he would scream and beg his parents for help. Now when he feels an attack coming on, Obi snuggles up to Christian on the sofa or in bed and just the warmth of his body seems to avert another and settle him right down.

Even Christian's studies have improved; he's more focused and motivated because he knows that if he gets his work done he's free to spend time with his dog. He's doing A levels and, when he finishes school, hopes to do a university course at home to study psychology so that he can help other children with autism.

'Obi has really helped our family unit,' says Sarah. 'As a teenager, Christian has had all the issues that most kids his age have – and more. He used to be really upset about not having many friends but now he takes it in his stride. With Obi, he has a friend who is unconditionally loyal. He doesn't have to worry about being someone he's not to impress him. And he knows that, unlike people, he won't ever judge him and he doesn't put him under pressure. Obi is an absolute cuddle monster who loves nothing more than being tickled on his tummy by Christian, yet the very act of doing this is so mutually beneficial for them both. I can feel the tension easing out of Christian when he's with his dog. He comes everywhere with us. We plan our holidays around taking him with us so he can run along dog-friendly beaches and have a vacation himself. He is such an important part of our family. I don't know where we would be without him.'

CHAPTER 8

YVONNE AND MILLY'S STORY

Yvonne was horribly depressed when it occurred to her that she could get a dog to keep her company. As a sufferer of unstable diabetes, which is the rarest form of the illness, she hardly left her house in Paisley, Scotland for fear of her blood sugar levels becoming dangerously low or high. Her body gave no warning that they fluctuated, and if they went to either extreme she would suffer a seizure which could lead to a coma and even death. She had lived an isolated life since her diagnosis in 1977 and her condition had worsened to the point where was barely able to control it.

If her blood sugar levels fell or peaked, Yvonne would slur her words, feel sweaty, sometimes tremble and suffer from headaches. The trouble was, these were common ailments and not just specific to diabetics, so it was difficult to be certain it was her blood sugar levels that were causing her symptoms. She therefore had to carry a blood glucose monitor with her at all times, so that she could instantly check her levels if necessary. To try to alleviate an extreme reading and to avoid a seizure, she would eat something sugary or get a drink.

'I had to give up work in 1993 because I'd pass out at work or have to take time off when I was ill,' says Yvonne. 'It was devastating for me because I loved my job working as a bookkeeper in my local theatre. Gradually, over the years, I gave up other important parts of my life too. I didn't go out as much with my friends because I could tell they were constantly worried about me. I've been out with them and suffered seizures, so they were always on guard watching me, which I didn't feel was fair so I stopped socialising altogether. I didn't want my seizure to be the main attraction when we were out at a wedding or a special dinner. My son Adam put a doorbell on my bedpost so that if I did feel like I was going to pass out, I could try to ring the bell before it happened to summon him into my room to help me. I didn't like doing this because I felt it was too much pressure on Adam, but it had to be done. I didn't always manage to alert him because my levels could change in an instant and with no warning. I felt like Adam wasn't being allowed to lead a normal life because he always had to take care of me. I wanted to look after myself but the nature of my diabetes means that it was difficult. Adam never complained about looking after me but I knew that my illness put restrictions on his life too and I hated it. Everywhere I went, he had to come with me and for a young man who should be enjoying himself out with his friends, it wasn't ideal. Because I was getting hypos, which are when my blood sugar levels fall dangerously low, most days, I couldn't even attend all of my health appointments like the doctor, dentist or podiatrist. I had to live day by day, never arranging anything, because I knew that the chances were that I'd have to change it. It became easier to shut myself away from the outside world and be by myself.'

Being so isolated was very depressing for Yvonne and she took tablets to help her cope with her loneliness. She didn't realise that she was so depressed; she just thought she was having anxiety issues that she could handle herself. It wasn't until she hit rock bottom that she thought about the possibility of getting a dog. Yvonne's previous dog had died seven years prior and she hadn't replaced her because she felt that her diabetes would prevent her from caring for an animal properly. However, she remembered and missed a dog's loyal companionship, so she hoped she could find a tiny dog who needed to be fostered or rescued. The more she thought about getting a dog, the more it made sense to her. It would have to be an older animal who was already trained rather than a puppy.

Yvonne scoured the Internet looking for rescue dogs, and came across the website of Medical Detection Dogs, a charity based in Milton Keynes. Their experts train dogs to identify the odour changes that are associated with medical conditions such as unstable diabetes and Addison's disease. The dogs are then able to alert their owners before they themselves are aware that they are about to fall ill; in a diabetic's case, they can then get themselves the appropriate treatment to avoid a life-threatening situation. It costs £10,000 to train one of their service dogs and the process, based on positive rewards for good behaviour, is rigorous.

Yvonne told a relative about the charity, and they suggested that she contact Medical Detection Dogs to see if she might be a suitable candidate to receive one of their animals. It looked too good to be true and Yvonne, still nervous about even getting a dog, put off sending her application form until six months later.

A tiny Yorkshire Terrier was going through her service dog training at MDD when Yvonne sent in her application. The little dog was given to the charity when a man left a cardboard box containing five eight-week-old puppies at the Wood Green Animal Shelter, having discovered them at the roadside. The puppies were emaciated and sickly, covered in faeces and with matted hair, but they were alive.

A staff member at the charity also volunteered at the Wood Green Animal Shelter and, as she worked with the pups, she felt that one in particular, Milly, would be suitable to become an MDD lifesaver. Dogs that are taken in by the MDD charity have to be confident and well adjusted to people – Milly ticked the right boxes. She found a home with MDD and spent the next 18 months being socialised with other dogs and humans, and being taught how to walk in every public situation imaginable so that she would be able to accompany her new owner anywhere without fear or worries.

When Yvonne finally applied to MDD, she was quickly matched with Milly, who had been taught to detect odour changes in diabetes sufferers. Yvonne was asked to send breath samples to the charity so that Milly could be taught to recognise her personal smells and identify when Yvonne's blood sugar levels went from one extreme to the other.

They met for a week's training, in November 2012, and the very first night that Milly stayed with Yvonne at her hotel, the clever canine put her skills to use.

'The first night she woke me up twice because my blood sugar levels were too high,' recounts Yvonne. 'She barked loudly and pawed me in bed, so I woke up. I tested my levels and they were high because I was stressed being away from home, so I took insulin and went back to sleep once I knew my levels were lower. A few hours later, it happened again and she woke me up again by getting in bed and licking my face, so I was able to take more action and avert a dangerous seizure. It was amazing to me because the sweet girl didn't even know me yet she potentially saved my life. I couldn't wait to get her home. Her trainers were thrilled that she was doing her job so well. She took to me straight away and from the start we were an amazing match. I still don't know how I got so lucky to have found her.'

Since Milly came into her life, Yvonne hasn't had a single seizure, which is quite remarkable considering that she was having debilitating seizures almost daily. The service dog goes everywhere with Yvonne: supermarket shopping, to buy clothes, and for walks to get some fresh air and a change of scenery. Yvonne now enjoys meeting up with friends and family for dinners and nights out. She feels comfortable enough to have fun because she knows that if her blood sugar levels fluctuate, Milly will alert her by jumping on her lap and putting her paws on her head.

'I wasn't living before I got Milly,' says Yvonne. 'I was somehow existing in my private little world. I wasn't seeing anybody except for my son because I chose to be alone. That way I wasn't a burden and I could live with my condition without bothering anybody. Now everyone knows Milly and they recognise when she's alerting me. It's great because they know to help me to sit down and to give me food or a drink. They can help me get my insulin out of my bag to make sure that I take it before I faint or have a seizure. Having this reassuring, calm little dog has given me the confidence to get out in the world, to see people again, to even do my own shopping again. Just getting out of the house is a huge thing for me. I'm managing my diabetes with my Milly and she makes all the difference. Apart from her practical talents, Milly is also great at cheering me up when I'm having a bad day. My depression is controlled because I only have to look at Milly and I can't help but smile. She might have had a difficult start but she's loved more than anything and I'm so thankful she's in my life. Milly is my hero.'

CHAPTER 9

EVELYN AND JERRY LEE'S STORY

Everyone hopes and dreams that they will meet the love of their life; that special someone who we can call our soulmate. However, if we're lucky enough to find our soulmate, their death can leave a deep, dark void that is a struggle to deal with. When Evelyn's husband Frank died, she wished she had died with him.

The couple met on a hot summer's day in Evelyn's home town of Duncanville, Texas, in July 1978. Their paths crossed at a time when she wasn't even looking for love.

'I was divorced and I honestly was quite happy doing my own thing, being on my own,' recalls Evelyn. 'I was taking the time to be myself, to find out what I wanted out of life. It was lunchtime and I was having a cup of iced tea in the local cafe, just a few doors down from the pharmacy where I worked at the time. I'll always remember that day because it was so balmy hot that the cafe was packed with people looking for cold drinks to cool off.'

At the table next to Evelyn sat a group of construction workers and she couldn't help but hear them talking about how they were building houses as part of a huge project for a large firm.

They all looked similar – dirty jeans and T-shirts, cargo boots and filthy faces – yet one stood out despite having his back to her.

'I could see this man's profile and I noticed he had a strong jawline and thick, dark hair that rested over the collar of his red and black plaid shirt,' says Evelyn. 'However, I noticed he said very little – he just nodded his head, sipped his drink and was quiet. I wondered what he was thinking about.'

This was a small town where everyone knew everyone else, but Evelyn hadn't seen the man in the plaid shirt before, so she thought he must be visiting from another town or from the city.

Evelyn finished her iced tea and went back to work. That afternoon was slow in the pharmacy but, a couple of hours later, the front doorbell rang and in walked the man in the plaid shirt, black jeans, brown heavy work boots and a grey cowboy hat.

'I recognised him immediately,' recalls Evelyn. 'And I remember thinking just how handsome he looked close up! I felt my cheeks go red when he came to the counter, smiling broadly at me.

He ordered some medication, which I later learned he didn't need – he was just looking for an excuse to come into the store. Then he asked me for my name and number so we could go out on a date. I was taken aback but there was something about this man who was stood in front of me. He had an honest face and he looked me right in the eye, so I felt as if I could see right inside him. Somehow, I knew instinctively that this was a good man.'

Evelyn gave the handsome stranger her phone number, something she had never done before. Despite their brief encounter, she knew that he was going to call her and that something special was about to happen.

She was right. After a whirlwind six-month courtship, the pair were married in January 1979. Evelyn and Frank were middle-aged divorcees who had fallen deeply in love and who weren't prepared to wait because they knew in their hearts that they had met their soulmates. They had taken a risk getting married so quickly but it was a risk that paid off.

Although a quiet man, Frank was kind and loyal, and from the moment he met Evelyn's family, he fitted right in. The couple spent many happy years together. Frank was what Evelyn called a 'fixer' – he could repair anything at all he put his hands to. This talent was just one of the things that Evelyn would miss when Frank was gone because he did everything for her, from wiring a plug to changing a car tyre. He looked after his girl as if she were a queen.

Sadly, over the years, Frank's health deteriorated when his diabetes became much worse and the medications stopped working. In the end, he ran out of strength to fight his disease and, a few days after Christmas 2006, he died of heart failure brought on by diabetes complications.

All of a sudden, Evelyn didn't have Frank to care for any more. She didn't have the man by her side who made her laugh, who told her how beautiful she was and how much he loved her with all his heart.

'I was devastated,' recounts Evelyn. 'While it was a relief that Frank wasn't in pain and suffering any more, I had never felt so alone in my life. Not even after my divorce all those years before. Nursing him had been a full-time job and then there I was, alone, rattling around our house, not knowing what to do with myself because everything reminded me of Frank and what I had lost. I had to sit in his chair in the living room or sleep on his side of the bed just to feel close to him, to smell him, to hear him in my thoughts and in my dreams. I was so desperately sad that I thought I would never come to terms with losing him. My grief ran so deep sometimes I couldn't catch my breath.'

Evelyn lost her zest for life and started to live in her bedroom, where she could still feel Frank's presence. She stopped preparing the home-cooked meals that Frank had loved so much because she couldn't be bothered to cook just for herself. Cooking became a chore where once it had been a labour of love for her husband.

She spent her days in bed watching television or reading, living off jars of peanut butter, bread, biscuits and crisps. The only exercise she got was when she walked down the stairs to the kitchen to get more supplies; and the only peace she got was when she slept, hoping that Frank might appear to comfort her in her dreams.

Evelyn's daughter and four grandchildren were desperately worried about her and tried to visit her every day or to coax her out of the house for a walk or a trip to the shops. It was a battle that they rarely won.

It wasn't until Thanksgiving 2007 that something happened to bring Evelyn back to life. That something was nothing short of a miracle in the shape of a small, scruffy terrier dog.

Evelyn was spending her first Thanksgiving holiday at the home of Frank's son, Frankie, and his wife Keran. They had insisted that they wouldn't take no for an answer, so Evelyn had made an effort to get out of her four walls and visit theirs.

While the men were watching the football on the TV, Keran had something to show Evelyn.

'Come and see what I've got,' she said, and together they walked into the main bathroom. 'What do you think about that?'

On the floor was an old towel, and lying on it was the most pathetic looking, ugliest terrier-type dog Evelyn had ever seen. His brown fur was matted in places, and there were scabs all over his body where he had rubbed his hair away, leaving red, raw skin. He had one large tooth that protruded from his mouth at an angle, raising his top lip into an Elvis Presley curl, while his other teeth were brown and dirty. He also smelled like he hadn't had a bath in years.

'Where did you find him?' Evelyn asked, as the poor dog shivered on the towel, as if frightened of the two humans standing in front of him.

'He lives in the neighbourhood, foraging for food,' said Keran. 'He always seems to come to my house, probably because I give him the scraps. I know he has a home but I'm guessing they don't look after him properly because he's always burrowing under their fence to get out.'

Evelyn gently patted the pathetic little dog.

'Well, his owners don't deserve to have a dog,' she said. 'Poor boy, what a state he's in.'

'I've cleaned him up the best I can,' said Keran sadly. 'But I think I'll have to take him home, even though I don't want to because it's clear they don't want him otherwise they would make sure he doesn't get out of their garden.'

Evelyn looked into the dog's sad eyes, which reflected back at her the awful life he led. She could tell this sweet boy wasn't loved; that he probably didn't even know what love was.

'Can I hold him?' she asked, and she scooped him into her arms, where he promptly rested his head under her chin. Despite his bath, he stank like rotting flesh from the open sores, but still Evelyn couldn't put him down.

Yet the dog wasn't theirs to hold or to keep, and she knew that Keran was going to have to return him to his family, so she reluctantly put him back on his towel and they left him with a bowl of food and a loving hug.

Evelyn couldn't get the young dog out of her mind after she returned home. Those big, brown, pleading eyes had definitely left their mark on her heart but, as he already had a home, there was nothing that she could do except pray that his owners looked after him better.

A week later, Keran called.

'Guess who I'm hugging?' she said. 'It's the dog from Thanksgiving!'

'Is he OK?' asked Evelyn, worried that something had happened to him.

'He escaped from his home and he came to me again,' Keran said. 'This time, I spoke to his owners and they were not nice people.'

Evelyn's heart sank at the thought that this little dog lived with people who truly did not care about him. It was no wonder he escaped from his home every chance he could get.

'They said I could keep him this time, or take him to the dog shelter,' continued Keran. 'But I can't keep him here with our three dogs – they're too territorial. I thought you might like him though, Mum.'

'It had never crossed my mind that I could take in the dog,' recalls Evelyn. 'I had put on more than 45 kg from sitting in bed all day, eating the wrong foods and not looking after myself properly. Although I loved the idea, how could I care for a dog properly if I couldn't be bothered to take care of myself? Yet the thought of having a living, breathing companion in the house to keep me company was very tempting, so I told Keran I would take him in. I was nervous and excited

 How could I care for a dog properly if I couldn't be bothered to take care of myself?

at the thought of the dog arriving. Just as I felt when I met Frank all those years ago, it felt like the right thing to do.'

The next morning, Keran turned up at Evelyn's house with the pup, who immediately ran into her house as if he had lived there all his life. He went straight into the living room and jumped in Frank's old chair, which became one of his favourite spots – in addition to Evelyn's lap or her bed at night-time.

She named him Jerry Lee, the first name that popped into her head, because his shock of hair that stood on end made her think of the singer Jerry Lee Lewis.

The two hit it off straight away. If Evelyn was having a bad day – and numerous were the days when the loneliness and sadness overwhelmed her – Jerry Lee would sit on her knee or by her side on the bed, head cocked as she talked about her Frank and how he would have loved Jerry Lee. He wouldn't move away from her until she told him to, particularly if she was crying. He would lick her tears from her cheeks and pull his goofy grin, as if to make her smile because he knew her heart was aching.

As the days went by, it was as if a black cloud had lifted over Evelyn's house. The mundane life she had been leading changed with the arrival of Jerry Lee.

For a start, she had to walk him twice a day, meaning she made it out into the sunshine and the fresh air on a regular basis, which helped to lift her moods. She has lost more than 45 kg because she takes more regular exercise and she cooks healthier foods for both of them. Mealtimes aren't as lonely since they eat together at the dinner table.

Although only she could understand him, Evelyn taught Jerry Lee to bark 'Mama' and 'I love you'. She swore that he tried to copy her when she spoke to him, and this made her laugh until she cried.

'Then one day, I realised I was laughing much more than I was crying,' recalls Evelyn. 'And I suddenly realised that Jerry Lee was helping me to come to terms with Frank's death – that he was the reason I was starting to live again. And it felt so good!'

Jerry Lee became Evelyn's best friend and protector. He was there when she needed a shoulder to cry on and he was also there to look after her when they were out walking. One day, they were enjoying their morning walk when a large white Pit Bull ambushed them as they walked past a neighbour's house. He ran so fast towards them, growling and snarling at them both, that as Evelyn tried to hurry past, she caught her heel in her long skirt and she fell into the road.

The Pit Bull made as if to attack Evelyn as she struggled to get up, which, being an older lady with arthritis, wasn't particularly easy. Jerry Lee jumped in between Evelyn and the Pit Bull, causing the other, much bigger dog to stop in his tracks while Jerry Lee barked in his face.

The two dogs faced off. Evelyn felt sure that Jerry Lee would come off far worse because of his size, yet the Pit Bull abruptly turned around and ran back into his garden, giving her time to get on her feet, with Jerry Lee guarding her. As Jerry Lee licked her face, there was no doubt that somehow he had saved her from a violent mauling despite him being the smaller animal.

Although she still misses Frank and always will, Evelyn now has someone else to take care of and to love.

'Jerry Lee has saved me in so many ways,' says Evelyn. 'I took him in and he will be forever grateful. He understands that and it's why he's so protective of me – he's thankful and he truly loves me as much as I adore him. He came into my life at a time when I needed a friend, someone to be there for me, to take the loneliness of losing Frank away. Jerry Lee is my rod – he has given back my purpose in life and, until I meet Frank again in Heaven, he will be my best friend and protector. Jerry Lee *is* my Frank. I swear Frank sent him to stand in for him, to pull me out of my depression and loneliness. I just don't know where I would be now without my little dog who has become my whole world. He has given me so much – he rescued me from myself and thanks to him, my story is so different to how it could have turned out. Jerry Lee, you're my world. We're so lucky our paths crossed.'

CHAPTER 10

REYA AND TIGA'S STORY

Julie was at the end of her tether when they found the light brindle-coloured dog on the Internet.

Her daughter Reya had been arrested again, this time for criminal damage, and she'd spent two long days in custody at the police station in Brighton. Reya fell off the straight and narrow years before, when she got in with the wrong crowd, and had been thrown out of several different schools for bad behaviour. Julie made a last-resort bargain with her wayward child: if she stopped getting in so much trouble, then maybe she could have the dog she so desperately wanted.

'I was out of control,' recalls Reya. 'I was rebellious and had no respect for authority. I didn't like anyone, I hated school and I just wanted to make trouble all the time. It didn't matter to me that I was destroying my life.'

It all started going wrong when Reya joined high school. She loved studying and got on well with her teachers, until she made friends with a girl who became a bad influence on her. Reya hated the restrictions of school and having to attend day after day, and she started to rebel by skipping school. At first she would go into the school building and just not turn up for class, then she wouldn't even bother turning up at school for the subjects she disliked.

Reya was terribly disruptive in the classes she did attend – she was loud, obnoxious and loved to start an argument. From not turning in homework to chatting loudly during class and shouting at her teachers, she craved attention, but it was the worst possible kind. At the age of 14, she was expelled from school.

'My mum was devastated,' says Reya. 'She was a single mum to me and my younger sister Faye and she had always done her very best for us. Me getting expelled was like she hadn't done her job as a mum properly and she took it very personally. She was upset and disappointed in me. I was the one who was going to do so well at school. I was bright and I had once had high grades, so when I was expelled it was shocking because, despite the fact she had done everything right, it obviously wasn't enough. All Mum wanted was to give me and Faye a good life and I was throwing it all back in her face. Looking back, I do wonder if I was a bit depressed at the time, with all my hormones racing and the pressure to do well, but even that's no excuse for the way I behaved.'

Reya started another school and she hated it too. She had no friends at first and she felt so alone. She was also incredibly angry that her mum had sent her back to school – she could not see that she was being given a second chance and that it was an opportunity to redeem herself. She skipped classes at her new school too because she hated being in that kind of environment. Her teachers here were more strict, which made her furious, so she would fly into rages in the classes that she did attend.

Things came to a head when she got into an argument with a teacher who was trying to calm her down and she smashed a noticeboard into the wall, shattering it completely and leaving a huge mark.

She was sent home and ordered to return the next day for a crisis meeting with her head teacher and her mother. Even though Julie pleaded her daughter's case in this meeting, she was expelled again.

Around the same time, Reya was getting into regular trouble with the police. She and her friends went out drinking in the streets, grabbing whatever they could to get drunk out of their minds. They were often arrested for being drunk and disorderly. Once, they spent the night in the cells after throwing a rubbish bin through a shop window for no reason – just because it was 'fun'. Reya escaped jail time but had to be monitored by a young offenders' team and had to send a letter of apology to the shopkeeper. A court judge placed a curfew on Reya so that if she wasn't in her house by 9 p.m., she could be arrested. The order infuriated her too so she refused to stick to it, much to her mum's anguish.

'I became arrogant,' says Reya. 'I'd walk out of the front door knowing my mum was in the living room. Then I'd boldly walk down the local high street, almost looking for a police officer to come and arrest me. I purposely tried to annoy people to get a rise out of them. I hated the police with a passion – to me, they were pigs and I had zero respect for them. It was nothing for me to swear at the police and lash out at them just because I could. My mum was so upset, I just don't think she knew what the heck to do with me. I'd go out of the house and then sneak back through the window later on or I'd stop at friends' houses. At the time I couldn't see a future for myself and I was living day by day, moment by moment. I'd given up the idea of ever going to university and having a career. I cared about nothing in my life, not even my mum and my sister, who were going through hell with me. I was in a very bad place.'

When Reya was 16, she was remanded in prison for two days. The police had caught her violating her curfew again – and this time, as a repeat offender, she was in an awful lot of trouble. Julie had finally had enough.

'If you do this again, I won't be the one to come and bail you out,' she told Reya tearfully. 'I can't keep doing this – and I won't. If you want to stay in jail then be my guest. I'm not helping you again.'

It was tough love, but Julie felt she had no choice, believing this was the only way she could help her daughter. Reya did listen to Julie and she did stay in the house more, although she still went out on drinking binges and got into trouble for being drunk in public places.

Around this time, Reya watched a TV show about dogs and decided that she wanted one of her own. The family had always had cats but never a dog, and the thought of owning a pooch really appealed to Reya. Julie wasn't having any of it, though.

'Why would I buy you anything?' Julie asked. 'You cause nothing but trouble for me and for yourself. I'm not rewarding you for that kind of behaviour.'

Reya was not going to take no for an answer and she pestered her mother for days, until Julie understood that this could be used to her advantage because a dog might be a very effective bargaining tool.

'If you really want a dog, then you have to stop getting into trouble with the police,' she told Reya. 'That's my final offer. You start behaving like a normal sixteen-year-old and perhaps you can have one. You need to prove to me that you can be grown up and ready to own a dog.'

Reya mostly kept out of trouble for the next few months and, apart from the odd skirmish, the thought of getting a dog reined her in. She spent several months trawling local rescue charities, looking for an unwanted pet.

She didn't find a dog that caught her eye until she saw an advert on the Pets 4 Homes website, which offered a six-month-old Staffordshire Bull Terrier cross for adoption. There were pictures of him with a cat and with his owner, so Reya was confident he would get on with her cats. She emailed the owner and still hadn't heard anything back after several days, so she emailed her again. There was just something about this dog's face and eyes that appealed to Reya and she felt instinctively that this boy was for her.

One night, she prayed intently that she would have this dog. The next day, she received a phone call from his owner to say that she hadn't been able to call because he had chewed through her phone lines!

Julie agreed that he looked like a nice hound, so she drove Reya and Faye to take a look at the animal. They weren't disappointed. As soon as they entered the house, the dog went straight up to Reya and followed her into the living room.

The dog hadn't experienced the most promising start in life. The runt of the litter, he'd had about five homes already and he was still such a baby. At a previous home they couldn't handle him because he was so boisterous, so they had asked his latest owner to take him in. She couldn't cope with his hyperactivity either, so she advertised to find him a new home. If no one contacted her, she was planning on taking him to the RSPCA.

Reya *knew* that she had to have this dog and she didn't think twice about the fact that he had been passed around so much that he was likely to have emotional problems. She wanted the friendly dog and, luckily for her, so did Julie and Faye.

They picked him up the next day. Reya named the dog Tiga and made him a bed in her bedroom; he attached himself to her like glue. It was very sweet but she soon found out that he'd had little or no training and truly was like a young puppy. She had to teach him toilet training from scratch. Walking him on the lead was a nightmare because he was so big and strong and he didn't know how to behave, so Reya read up about training on the Internet and spent much time and energy on getting him under control.

For four months, Reya didn't leave her dog, so she didn't get into trouble. She rarely went out – only to walk him. When her friends texted her to ask her to go out drinking, she replied that she couldn't leave her Tiga. For the first time in her life, Reya cared about something other than herself. Seeing Tiga make progress was such a reward in itself that she wanted to spend every waking moment with him. He was like an addiction but a very healthy one.

'When we first got Tiga he was very insecure and nervous and I guess I saw myself in him,' says Reya. 'I think that we bonded so well because we were the same – we were both scared and lost and we didn't know where we were going. Having such a responsibility taught me huge lessons. I quickly made a vow not to get into trouble and have to spend time in jail because in my mind he'd think I'd abandoned him, and who would've looked after him the way I did? No one. I couldn't do anything to risk that and as his confidence and self-esteem grew, so did mine. I got a thrill out of seeing him behave and accomplish a command. He truly gave me something much more important to think about. I even stopped being so angry all the time. I remember once, I was furious about

For the first time in her life, Reya cared about something other than herself

something and I shouted so loud, he ran away and cowered behind a chair, shaking horribly. It was enough to bring me to my senses because I realised how scared and disappointed in me he must have been. I vowed never to be like that around him again.'

Tiga was with Reya every step of the way while she studied hard in her bedroom for her GCSEs and A levels in preparation for her health sciences course at college. They have transformed each other's lives and the pair are still never far apart.

'Tiga was a huge wake-up call for me,' Reya says. 'He came into my life at a time when I needed him; I needed something or someone to shake me up and make me see that I was going down an awful path. He saved my life. Four years ago I thought that I was heading for a lifetime in and out of jail. I didn't think I'd go to college and I didn't have any ambitions to do well. I thought I'd probably end up pregnant or even dead. Now with Tiga by my side, I know that anything is possible. With him to keep me grounded, I don't think I'll ever go back to that dark place ever again. He's my shining light and I hope I'm his too.'

CHAPTER 11

--- --- --- --- --- --- --- --- --- --- --- --- --- ---

KATHRYN AND BOUDI'S STORY

Kathryn was ambitious, career-minded and had planned out the next few years of her life in great detail. Ten years previously, she had left her childhood home in the Northern Irish countryside to study in London. Life in the capital was every bit as exciting and fulfilling as she'd hoped when she took the plunge to leave behind everything and everyone she knew to pursue her dreams.

After graduating from college, Kathryn studied journalism and enjoyed several jobs on different magazines as a financial correspondent. She took a few months out to work in Dubai editing two magazines before returning to London, homesick for her friends and the city she loved so much.

In London, she enjoyed an enviable lifestyle. While she was working hard and rising quickly through the ranks, Kathryn spent her evenings with friends at little bistros and restaurants or watching movies. She lived in a flat in East London with

Kate, a burlesque dancer from Australia, and she would spend hours at the theatre watching her friend dance in shows. Life was so hectic that there was never time to feel lonely – and life was good.

At the beginning of 2013, Kathryn took a promotion with one of the biggest national news agencies, where she was hired as a financial editor. This meant more hours in the office and frequent visits to press briefings at Whitehall plus the opportunity to report on the nation's trends and financial concerns. It was a job Kathryn excelled at and loved, so when she was called into the office a few months later to speak to her boss, she was expecting a friendly chat about her upcoming assignments.

She couldn't have been more wrong. Her boss calmly told her that he was very sorry but they 'had to lose her' – she was out of a job with immediate effect. Kathryn cleared out her office, her carefully laid plans for her future in total ruins.

'The redundancy was completely unexpected,' recalls Kathryn. 'I had no indication it was coming. Only the week or so before I'd had an evaluation of my work and I was told I was doing a fantastic job. There was no notice. I had to leave the office there and then. It almost felt like I was fired, even though I obviously wasn't. I think that they had created the post for me but then they couldn't afford me, so I had to go. I was devastated. I called my friend who was working at Buckingham Palace at the time and she met with me straight away. I was in floods of tears, I was shell-shocked and I just didn't know what the heck I was going to do next. Suddenly, it felt as if I had lost a career I loved and the future I had hoped and planned for was never going to happen. It was like I was living a nightmare and there was nothing I could do about it. I'd worked so hard to get into journalism. For me, it wasn't just a career, it was a vocation, and I was really good at it. It didn't make sense that they were letting me go because they couldn't fault my work. It was so unfair.'

To make matters worse, Kathryn had just put an offer in on her first home, a two-bedroom flat in Dalston, East London. She had been planning to stay at her new job for at least five years, and she had been hunting for a suitable place to buy in order to get her feet on the property ladder at an early age. Her mortgage had been approved in an area of London where she would be surrounded by friends, but now she had to withdraw her offer. She was heartbroken.

Feeling defeated, Kathryn flew home to her parents, David and Geraldine, in County Down, desperate for them to tell her what to do and how to deal with her redundancy. It was decided that she would return to her family home in Northern Ireland for a while so that she could get her head together and work out what to do next.

Two weeks later, Kathryn and her dad flew to London and packed up all of her worldly belongings in a few boxes, then they hired a van and took a ferry to Belfast. It was an emotional departure for Kathryn as she was saying goodbye to her housemate Kate and friends she had known since her college days, but she was also bidding farewell to a city she loved more than anywhere else in the world, somewhere she had thought she might live for most of her life.

With no warning, she had lost her job, her home and her friends. Although she was grateful to her parents for helping her, she had to adjust to being back in her childhood bedroom at her parents' house.

'While it was a relief to have somewhere to run to, on the other hand it wasn't good to be having to go back to a place I had left behind over a decade before,' says Kathryn. 'I felt as if I was returning home as a huge failure. I'd never imagined I'd ever go back to the place I left all those years before because I thought that London had more opportunities for me. I couldn't imagine what opportunities I could ever find in Northern Ireland. I was a financial journalist, which is a specialist position. London was a hub of everything that I loved and wanted in my life. Being stuck living at home with my parents certainly wasn't what I had planned to be doing ever again.'

Kathryn has suffered on and off with depression and anxiety for most of her life and she has learned to recognise the symptoms. It didn't take long, with all the emotional upheaval and stress, for her to fall into a dark place. She cried most of the time, unable to function or think clearly. She struggled to make any major decisions about her career or what she wanted to do with her future because she couldn't see past what she deemed a huge failure. She struggled to find a new purpose. Kathryn questioned her ability as a journalist and sometimes even imagined that she must have been to blame for what happened. She slept a lot, barely getting out of bed before midday. It felt as if she was floating with nowhere to go.

A doctor diagnosed Kathryn with depression and suggested that, while she was in the safety of her parents' house, she should take time out to get her head straight and to come to terms with what had happened. She signed on the dole, which was deflating for Kathryn as she had never been without a job before and had never been without money of her own. However, she was in no fit state to even apply for a job.

Kathryn had lost her motivation and sense of ambition. She couldn't see a way out of her sad, pathetic state until, one September morning, she was talking to her parents in their room, when she spotted an animal in the driveway. The family home is deep in the countryside and at first she couldn't make out what the white streak of fur sniffing around was. Her initial thought was to shoo away the animal, which looked a bit like a pig. The family had just taken in an unwanted cat and Kathryn didn't want this animal to get into the house and chase or bother it.

As Kathryn walked towards it, the animal gingerly ran over to her and rolled over onto her back. To Kathryn's surprise, it was a little brown-and-tan-coloured dog like a Jack Russell Terrier and, as she was friendly, Kathryn thought she must have escaped from her home.

There was no one in the country lane looking or shouting for the dog, so Kathryn took her and went to the houses in her street to see if she belonged to anyone. No one had seen her before and, as she wasn't wearing a collar, Kathryn didn't have much to go on.

She took her to the vet to see if she was microchipped – again, no clues. The vet examined the dog and said that she was likely to be aged between three and six years old and, as her teats were swollen, it looked like she had been feeding puppies recently. The vet also said that judging by the number of scratch marks and wounds on her head and all over her body, she was probably a breeding dog who had been dumped because she was too old to breed from any more, or she wasn't producing enough puppies. This was a common occurrence and the dogs, if they survived at all, often ended up in a shelter where they would be lucky to get adopted out because they usually had health issues and severe emotional trauma.

Kathryn took her home and called the dog warden for her area. She also posted photos of the dog on her Facebook and Twitter accounts, asking for help in locating her owner, but no one knew who she was or where she had come from.

After three months, with her parents' blessing, Kathryn adopted the sweet girl and called her Boudi. The two had formed a strong bond already and, for the first time in weeks, Kathryn had stopped dwelling on losing her job. She threw her energies into looking after Boudi, who evidently needed Kathryn to feel loved and settled.

From the start Boudi was very clingy, following Kathryn absolutely everywhere she went. When anyone raised their voice in the house, Boudi would cower and tremble, suggesting that she had been beaten in the past. Initially, she didn't like being stroked at all and it took Kathryn days to persuade her that she wasn't going to hurt her.

She didn't bark for more than six months, so Kathryn had her vocal cords examined by a vet, who said that they were perfectly healthy. They assumed that at the breeding facility where she had lived before, she was severely punished if she had barked, so she had stopped altogether.

While Boudi blossomed in such a caring, loving atmosphere, Kathryn began to feel better too.

'Boudi was the only creature I came across who was in a worse shape than I was,' reminisces Kathryn. 'I was depressed and feeling so sorry for myself, then along came Boudi, who was vulnerable and completely lost. She put everything into some sort of perspective for me. Suddenly, I went from sleeping all the time and crying to having to get up in the morning for Boudi. I had to take care of her because if I didn't, no one else would and she deserved to be loved. I realised for the first time that I couldn't dwell on my own misery and in order to look after her I had to take care of myself. And she was so responsive to any affection, be it a pet on the head or a tight hug, that it was impossible not to feel joy when she was around me. There was no way I couldn't be happy seeing her thrive because of my love and attention. Just taking her out for walks in the fresh air was so good for me. No matter how depressed I was feeling, once I got out of the house with Boudi and cleared my head, I would return home in a much better, happier mood. I remember how one

it was impossible not to feel joy when she was around me

day, during a walk, she suddenly ran down a field as fast as she could as if she was so happy to be alive and to be free to run. Watching her run at full pelt made my heart soar and, even today, watching her run with not a care in the world gives me so much joy.'

Within a few months of Boudi's appearance, Kathryn's depression was clearing and she felt in a position to start to plan her new future. It was a huge step for her, one she would never have been able to take without Boudi by her side. She bought a car and moved to south Belfast, where she rented a house for a while, and she returned to journalism but as a full-time freelancer. It didn't take long for her career to restart and now she is busy again, which is just how she likes it.

When she moved house with Boudi, she reconnected with old school friends, which kick-started her social life. Kathryn bought her first house, a lovely three-bedroom terrace with a small garden for half the money that she had been going to spend on her London flat.

Kathryn is also in the best shape of her life. She met her personal trainer, a former marine called Jack, at the park when she was walking Boudi and he was there with his Yorkie dog,

Maximus. The two became friends and now she exercises with him every week. She has made many other friends because of Boudi and their walks. She says that she has come full circle and is in a great place in her life right now.

'Boudi saved me from myself,' says Kathryn. 'She appeared at a time when I needed her the most. I was struggling with such a huge depression and she was the catalyst I needed for me to get myself sorted out. She gave me a reason to get going, to do more things and once I did, I remembered what I had been missing. I remembered what being happy was really like, how I loved being busy and how much I valued my job. My dog goes everywhere with me. She sleeps with me, she's always there when I need a hug and a shoulder to cry on. When I met my boyfriend Jack (not the personal trainer) two years ago, I decided that if she approved, then he was a good guy – Boudi loves him! Boudi has given me so much love and attention. She saved me and I'm glad she found her way into my life that day. That little dog changed my life in so many ways for the better and I know one thing: while she's with me I'll never be lonely with my own dark thoughts again.'

CHAPTER 12

MOLLY AND ALFIE'S STORY

Starting a new school was extremely tough for Molly. She suffered a stroke during her birth and the resulting brain injury meant that the left side of her body was much weaker. She walked with a slight limp, her left arm turned in slightly and her left hand was a little smaller than the other. Molly was becoming increasingly self-conscious about her differences, feeling that they made her stand out from her peers, but in her 11 years she had defied all expectations – when she was born, in Florida, doctors had warned her parents, Sharon and David, that she may never walk or lead a normal life.

'It was devastating,' recalls Sharon. 'To hear that our beautiful baby daughter might never walk and may be in a wheelchair for the rest of her life was the worst thing that, as a parent, you can ever imagine hearing. I cried for days.'

Hours of physical therapy paid off and, from age five, Molly had shown a keen interest in basketball, growing into a talented player who could run like the wind, her limp barely noticeable, dribble with the best and shoot like a pro. She also learned to ride a horse at an early age and this helped her with balance issues. Despite her physical disadvantages, Molly had a determined personality and possessed a strong will to succeed. The brain damage caused only physical limitations and her intelligence was unaffected. She was as bright as a button and excelled at school.

Leaving the familiar environment of primary school and starting middle school made both Molly and Sharon nervous. One of Sharon's major worries was that Molly would struggle to get to her classes on time because the new school was much bigger and would involve a lot more walking.

'When she rushes and tries to go fast, especially if she's tired, her limp becomes more obvious and she stumbles and falls,' says Sharon. 'I was afraid that she would take a tumble and fall and hurt herself. Or that the kids would laugh at her.'

Thankfully, Molly made some nice friends who helped carry her books between classes. She started to talk about school all the time and how much she loved her subjects and teachers, which was a blessing to her mum's ears.

Just a couple of months later, something changed. Molly asked Sharon to take her to school in the car rather than getting the bus because, she claimed, she didn't like getting up earlier to catch the bus. Sharon couldn't take her every day due to work commitments, and on the days that Molly was supposed to take the bus, she would complain of a stomach ache or cause an argument in order to miss the bus.

'I let her stay home a few times, gave her the benefit of the doubt,' says Sharon. 'But then when the stomach aches became much more frequent, I realised that I wasn't being told the whole story. I asked her time and time again if there was something wrong at school, but each time she said no and that she just didn't feel well. I know my daughter and I didn't believe her. I knew there was something else going on.'

Molly's attitude altered. She went from an outgoing, happy young lady who had something to say about everything to a quiet, withdrawn child who had lost her zeal for life. Sharon asked her over and over if anyone was upsetting her at school and Molly always denied this. Sharon asked her teachers if anything was going on, but they were as in the dark as she was.

As the weeks merged into each other, Molly seemed to lose her will to carry on. She would get home from school and retire to her bedroom to read, so she said, or she would lie for hours listening to music. Sometimes she would emerge from her room with red eyes, like she had been crying, but this was always denied.

Perhaps the most telling clue that something was wrong was when Molly gave up playing basketball in the garden. She used to shoot hoops every day after school but stopped this habit, using the excuse of too much homework. She became obsessed with her walking exercises – Sharon caught her several times practising walking straight like a 'normal person' and not with a limp.

One day, in the car on the way to school, Molly burst into tears.

'Please don't make me go to school today, Mum,' she cried. 'I can't go in today. I just can't.'

Sharon pulled the car in to the side of the road and Molly cried as if her heart was going to break.

'They keep asking me why I walk funny,' she sobbed. 'They keep following me and walking with a limp, pretending to be me. They say that I'm lopsided and that I'm weird to look at. One girl keeps saying over and over that I'm disabled and I should be in a special school with all the other freaks.'

Molly revealed that three girls in her PE class tormented her every day they were in class together. They would poke her, call her names, ridicule her in low voices so the teachers wouldn't hear. She also told Sharon about two boys in the year above who took the same bus and would laugh loudly and call her a spastic every time she got on. Molly felt her differences more keenly now than ever; Sharon struggled to contain her anger and sadness.

'As a mum our nature is to nurture and protect,' recalls Sharon. 'I put my arms around Molly and I hugged her tight. I wanted to hurt those bullies so much, I really did. I told her that she wasn't a freak and she definitely wasn't disabled. I told her that these people were ignorant bullies who had to be stopped or they might hurt someone else the way they upset her.'

Sharon dropped Molly off at school and went to speak to the head of year, who promised that with the school's zero tolerance policy for bullies, the matter would be swiftly dealt with, which it was. However, Molly wasn't the same and she didn't bounce back as her parents expected her to. She seemed shut away in her own secret little world, which wasn't healthy for a young schoolgirl.

'I felt that we were quickly losing Molly,' says Sharon. 'I was terrified that she was in a dark place where she was depressed, and those thoughts scared the hell out of me. David and I knew we had to do something drastic to bring our gorgeous girl back, but the question was: what on earth could we do that would make a difference? That's when I had a brainwave.'

> **We had to do something drastic to bring our gorgeous girl back**

The previous summer, Molly had asked for a puppy. Her parents had said no because the family already owned an enormous St Bernard dog called Elton John and they didn't feel there was room for another. Sharon read an article about the healing influence of dogs on their owners and, the more she thought about it, the more she realised that perhaps getting Molly a pet could be the solution. Christmas was just a month away and Sharon decided that if Molly still wanted a dog, then she would have one.

One afternoon after school, Sharon did a detour and drove Molly to the local dog shelter. It was a wonderful adoption facility with an impressive track record of finding homes for all of their strays. For the first time in months, Molly showed an interest in something.

'Why are we here?' she asked.

'You know you wanted a puppy?' her mum said. 'Well, let's see if we can find one here. A dog can be your Christmas present if you still want one.'

Molly's face was transformed in an instant and for the first time in ages Sharon saw a sparkle of life in her eyes. They walked into the shelter, which was beautifully maintained and clean. They followed the signs into the adoption room, where there were 12 cages on each side of the room, all occupied. The noise of the barking dogs was deafening as the animals – some scared, some alarmed at being in strange surroundings, others genuinely pleased to see strangers – greeted Molly and Sharon.

In the first cage to the right was a small, two-year-old dog called Pete. He was a sandy, terrier-looking dog of about 9 kg with bright brown, sparkling eyes and long eyelashes. The moment he saw Molly peer into his cage, he came running and licked her fingers through the bars. He was a scruffy little pup with a tail that didn't stop wagging, and he brought a huge smile to Molly's face as she petted his head through the bars and looked into his eyes.

 He was a scruffy little pup with a tail that didn't stop wagging

Pete had lived in a huge dog shelter in Georgia for

eight months but a fire burned it to the ground; only Pete and a handful of other dogs were rescued from the blaze that cost the lives of over 20 animals. Pete was taken in at this shelter after the fire and he had lived there for six months, so he was getting to be a bit of an old timer. The poor boy had been without a loving family for much of his life thus far. Despite all this, Pete was a sweet, friendly dog and he made an impression on Molly, who liked him as soon as she saw him. There was no denying how cute he was, so it was a bit of a mystery as to why he had been in shelters for so long.

Molly and Sharon walked around the shelter and met every dog. Some cowered in the back of their cages, too traumatised to say hello; others jumped up and down, overwhelmed with excitement, as if to say, 'Take me, take me!'

Molly decided that she wanted Pete but as Sharon filled out all the paperwork, the lady behind the counter showed them photographs of the most darling Jack Russell puppies who were due in the shelter the following week.

'Kids like you love puppies,' the woman said, smiling. 'Have a look at these little beauties before you make up your mind.'

There was no denying this either – those puppies were adorable and Molly could have had her pick. In the end, she put her name down for Pete and Cowboy, a tiny, sandy-and-tan-coloured pup with little ears and even shorter legs. She reserved both dogs and had a week in which to make her decision; Molly would have taken both, but there was only room for one in their household.

A week later, the family was approved for adoption and Molly had to decide who she wanted to bring home.

'I felt sure that she was going to pick Cowboy,' says Sharon. 'That puppy was just so gorgeous. Pete was older and, although adorable, he didn't have as much "cute factor" as this one did. But when we got to the shelter, Molly chose Pete. I was surprised but when she explained why she wanted him, I understood. She said that she knew Cowboy would find a home because he was a puppy, but she wasn't convinced that Pete, being older, would find a home so quickly, so she wanted him. I cried when she said that. I was so proud of her and that's when I knew deep in my heart that adopting Pete was the best thing we could ever have done for our Molly.'

Pete didn't answer to his name, so Molly changed his name to Alfred – Alfie, for short. This scruffy little dog, with a long body, short stubby legs and fur sticking out everywhere, might not have been the best looking pup in the world but he fitted right into his new home. A strong bond was quickly established between the pair.

Every night he slept with Molly, usually on her bed. From the outset, Alfie followed Molly everywhere as if he knew that it was she who had rescued him. She only had to call his name and he would be right there beside her, tail wagging with excitement. Molly took him out for walks twice a day, before and after school. This was a challenge at first because he hated wearing a collar, but Molly's kindness and perseverance taught him that a collar wouldn't hurt him.

After school and homework, Molly spent all her time with him. She taught him how to sit and roll over for a biscuit, to bark on command and to high-five her hand with his paw when he did something good. While Alfie was always obedient, there were certain things he would do only for Molly, such as sit on her lap when she called his name.

There was just one thing that Alfie wouldn't allow: he didn't like to be kissed. If you put your face next to him, he would turn, look in the opposite direction and shake, as if he expected to be beaten. It took several months, but one day Alfie licked Molly's face and let her kiss his, as if he was relearning to trust a human and Molly was the one who had earned his trust.

As the weeks went by, Molly's moods started to improve. She stopped the punishing walking exercises and didn't shut herself away in her room for hours on end. With a young dog to take care of, she didn't have time to focus on what may have set her apart from other people.

Molly went to school every morning in a much happier frame of mind. The bullies still made fun of her from to time, but she seemed stronger and better equipped to cope with it.

'I don't really care any more,' she confided to her mum. 'I ignore them and get on with what I'm doing. I don't let them get to me any more. I come home, see my lovely boy Alfie, take him for a walk and I just forget. Alfie needs me to look after him – and he needs me to be happy.'

Not long after his adoption, Alfie was playing in bushes near the barn where Molly rode horses, when he was run over by a hit-and-run motorist. After an hour-long search by the whole family, the poor boy limped home, every bone in his body shaking and crying his heart out. It turned out that his left hind leg was badly broken and it was touch-and-go whether he would pull through. Molly spent many hours caring for Alfie, nursing the life back into him.

Alfie did make it, although he was left with a limp, just like Molly's limp in her left leg. Dog and owner were now dealing with the same walking issues.

Adopting Alfie made all the difference to Molly's life. He brought her back from a place so dark that her parents wondered if they would ever see their daughter again.

'I'd watch Alfie with his limp playing with Molly in the garden, running and fetching things, and I couldn't help thinking that it was like watching a miracle happen before our eyes,' says Sharon. 'A miracle of hope, love and trust. It was like some sort of divine intervention happened where these two were supposed to meet so that they could help each other through their personal battles, so that they were never alone in their fights. I have no doubt that Alfie rescued my daughter from the brink, from an overwhelming depression

it was like watching a miracle happen before our eyes

and a serious lack of confidence in herself, but she also rescued Alfie by restoring his faith in humanity and allowing him the confidence to love again.'

Molly remains a determined, A-grade student, who has won her coveted place on her school's basketball team several years in a row. For extra practice for the try-outs, Molly and Alfie would run up and down the garden together to strengthen her leg and arm. All this training helped strengthen his weak leg too and Alfie is now completely healed.

'Alfie was and continues to be my inspiration,' says Molly. 'He was brought into my life at a time when I was at my lowest, when I thought everything was going wrong and I was a failure. He gave me that extra nudge when the going got tough to pull myself together and to start to respect and love myself for the person I am, rather than who I felt I should be. I may have rescued him from the shelter but he rescued me in many more ways from a dark and dismal place that could have destroyed me. I'm so thankful we found each other.'

CHAPTER 13

TRE AND EMBER'S STORY

Tre set eyes on the pretty Pit Bull dog at an animal adoption drive, an event organised by a charity to publicly showcase the dogs available for adoption, in his home town of Monroe, Cincinnati, and was instantly drawn to her. It was the way the beautiful white-and-tan dog looked at him kindly and wagged her long tail and her sloppy puppy kisses that did it for ten-year-old Tre. The family's beloved dog, a Pit Bull called Derby, had died a few months before, and Tre and his dad Tony were out looking for another pet to fill the huge gap she had left. It was June 2014 and the pair had gone to the Adore-A-Bull Rescue's open day, where the non-profit group was actively seeking homes for unwanted animals.

'Derby died of old age and I'd had her since college, so I was heartbroken,' says Tracy, Tre's mother. 'She was such a terrific dog, particularly around Tre and his younger sister Tycen. Pit Bulls have such an awful reputation for being vicious but Derby was the sweetest animal I'd ever known, very gentle and loving. When she died it was difficult for me to imagine us with another dog. When Tre and Tony came back from the adoption drive and they told me about this one dog, I still didn't know if I was ready to welcome a new pet into our home. Derby's passing was one of the most difficult things I've ever had to cope with. But everyone else wanted another Pit Bull because we had such a great experience with Derby, so I agreed to go and look at the dog just to appease the rest of the family. I didn't think we would actually bring her home.'

The dog had been taken out of the shelter by a foster mum who said that she had been in there for some time with her sister, who died from Parvo, a serious viral disease that is virtually incurable in dogs. She was a timid dog who had obviously not had much human contact. She had spent many days confined to her kennel at the shelter before Adore-A-Bull Rescue found her when she was around six months old.

She was such a sweetheart with Tre and Tycen. They played with her and she was so full of life, but crucially not too boisterous. She rested her head in their hands and Tracy knew instinctively that they had found the dog for them. She couldn't possibly say no to Tre.

They called the dog Ember and she settled into the family's busy lifestyle with ease. She made Tre her human. She slept on his bed at night and followed him around the house like his shadow. Wherever one was, the other wasn't too far behind.

Tre took his responsibility very seriously and spent many hours training and playing with Ember, so it was no wonder that they quickly bonded. She clearly adored him – you could see by the look in her eyes when he called her name – and it was good to see Tre so happy.

There was nothing Ember wouldn't do for her best friend – something that she proved in spectacular fashion almost a year after she was adopted.

In the early hours of a Sunday morning in May 2015, everyone in the house was asleep until Tracy woke up to a low-pitched growling, as if a wild animal was in her bedroom. Tracy jumped out of her skin when she opened her eyes to see what was wrong. Ember was sitting next to her side of the bed, making the most peculiar noise. It wasn't like she was growling in anger; it was a more distinct, urgent noise that grew louder as Tracy moved to get out of bed. It was obvious that she was trying to tell her something important.

'When I woke up and I saw her there, almost in my face and growling, I thought maybe she needed the toilet,' says Tracy. 'Although it was odd because she never got up to go out in the night. She was very good like that, so I wondered if she might have an upset stomach. I put on my house shoes so I could take her to the back door, but as we went into the hallway, she ran into Tre's bathroom, which was a few doors down from my bedroom. I followed her in and, to my horror, all I could see were Tre's legs hanging over the side of the bathtub. There

 There was nothing Ember wouldn't do for her best friend

was no water in the tub, thank God, but he was having a grand mal epileptic seizure so he was thrashing around like crazy. I'd never seen anything like that before and I screamed for my husband to come and help. It was the most frightening thing I've ever seen.'

Tre was rushed by ambulance to the Cincinnati Children's Hospital. He'd always been so healthy and there was no history of seizures in the family, so this incident was a huge scare for Tracy and Tony. At the hospital, doctors carried out a battery of tests to find out the cause of the seizure. Tre remembered nothing when he came round, so his doctors had to piece together what may have happened. They told Tre's frightened parents that he had probably felt unwell in the night, which is common just before a person has a seizure, and got up to go to the bathroom to be sick. He then had the seizure and fell into the bath, which is when Ember raised the alarm.

All the tests came back normal and his doctors declared that it was just one of those things, so Tre was allowed to return home. However, his own paediatrician would not accept that this was a one-off, random event, so she ordered more tests to make certain. A few months later, an MRI scan showed that Tre was suffering from epilepsy.

He now takes two tablets a day to control his condition. It's been tough for the family to cope with the restrictions of his illness. They have always been very sporty and now they have to be careful about what activities Tre takes part in, but they have adapted and Ember has been a huge part of his recovery. Ember follows the boy around the house and garden, watching over him constantly so that she can alert Tracy if he has another seizure. When he isn't feeling well, Ember is always there for a cuddle, something that keeps Tre happy and content. In the midst of this frightening health scare, Ember is a constant and the family thinks of her as their saviour.

'Ember keeps a very close eye on Tre,' says Tracy. 'He's had a couple of seizures since then, so we keep a monitor in his room at night to make sure we hear or see anything that happens. Whenever we look, Ember is curled beside Tre in bed and she's right up close. She follows him everywhere and I know that if anything happens, she'll come running to get me, so I feel safer letting him out of my sight. She's a great security blanket, plus she's company for Tre when he's not feeling well and he's stuck at home. Ember saved his life that night. I can't even begin to think what could have happened if she hadn't alerted us. She's not a trained service dog – she just does it instinctively and I'm sure it's her way of thanking us for rescuing her. She's an incredible member of our family.'

CHAPTER 14

ANDREA AND KILO'S STORY

Andrea had never seen herself as a dog owner but it's strange how things turn out. She'd always been a 'cat person' and it seemed to her that dogs needed so much more attention. When Andrea met her dog-loving partner Kevin and they eventually moved in together in Wakefield, Yorkshire, she had to get used to sharing a home with his four-legged friends, particularly because Kevin bred them for a business.

Gradually, Andrea fell in love with the animals, particularly Kevin's prized Staffordshire Bull Terriers, Buster and Holly, and one of their pups, Kilo. The pup was black and tan, and had the smoothest coat Kevin had ever seen or felt. Traditionally Staffies have rather coarse fur but Kilo's was as soft and as shiny as silk. As soon as Kilo could stumble around, he made a beeline for Andrea. It was as if the little dog had singled her out to be his mother.

However, it wasn't to be, because Kilo already had a home lined up for when he was old enough to leave his real mother. When Kilo went to his new home, at eight weeks old, Andrea was heartbroken but she knew it was for the best. Two big dogs in the house was more than enough, yet she missed the little furball, with his waggy tail and the velvet kisses.

Fate stepped in when Kilo was eight months old. Someone had mentioned to Kevin that Kilo's new owners were mistreating him, so Kevin and Andrea went to investigate; even when his dogs went to new homes, Kevin felt that he had an obligation to make sure they were being well looked after.

It transpired that Kilo was being kept all alone in a tiny shed in the garden. The previously bouncy ball of fluff was now so desperately thin that he seemed but a shadow of his former self, and the poor little thing was covered in fleas and what looked like bite marks.

Faced with such a pitiful sight, there was no way that Kevin was going to leave the puppy there in that hovel.

'If you're having problems looking after him, I'll take him back,' he told the owners. 'It's no problem.'

Despite the wretched state the dog was in, Kilo's owners didn't want to give him up. However, they agreed to take him to the vet the next day in order to get his fleas and the bites examined. While he was there, the vet discovered a horrific, infected sore underneath his fur, from the base of his tail all along his spine, where he'd been scratching at the fleas; Kilo must have been in terrible pain. The vet advised that Kilo would need a lot of specialist care and attention to tend to his wounds.

The very next morning, Kilo's owners turned up at Kevin and Andrea's house with the puppy.

'You can have him back,' they said. 'We can't afford to keep him.'

Kilo had come home. He quickly settled back into his old life, following Andrea everywhere and enjoying night-time cuddles on the sofa in front of the television.

Andrea suffers from mental health problems and she became increasingly reliant on Kilo. It seemed that every time she felt depressed or upset, he was there for her; a source of comfort in a world of emotional pain. She would sit for hours on the sofa or in bed with patient little Kilo, who wouldn't get up unless she did. If she cried, he would reassure her by snuggling into her neck, as if to let her know that she wasn't alone and that she was going to be OK with him by her side.

However, the good times were short-lived as there was another twist in the road ahead. When Kilo was the tender age of 18 months, Kevin and Andrea split up. Kevin moved out, leaving Andrea in a terrible state – but leaving her with the precious little dog.

Andrea couldn't function. She cried all the time, and her anxiety and depression quickly took hold, until she couldn't think about a life without Kevin. She felt that if she wasn't with the love of her life, then nothing was worth carrying on for. Andrea was so low that she even contemplated suicide, and if Kilo hadn't been there, she probably would have taken her life.

Things became so bad that Angela called for help and she was rushed to a mental health hospital, where she was sectioned to stay indefinitely.

'I had never felt so depressed,' recalls Andrea. 'I was at rock bottom and I couldn't think straight. I came to the conclusion that without Kevin my life wasn't worth living. I admit that I thought about ending it all right there and then. But as I cried and cried, Kilo came and sat on my lap. He looked me straight in the eye, as if he was pleading with me not to do anything stupid. He looked so sad himself that I couldn't do it. I realised I couldn't leave him because he loved me so much. He's the reason I decided to get help that night. I'm so glad that I did.'

The doctors concluded that Andrea had suffered a nervous breakdown. She ended up staying in hospital for four months, during which time she underwent counselling and took a course of antidepressants.

Despite Andrea being in the best possible hands, Kevin could not just stand by and watch her suffering. He knew how much Kilo meant to her so he often smuggled Kilo into Andrea's room to cheer her up. Kilo was definitely the best medicine. She looked forward to seeing her friend – the anticipation improved her mood and encouraged her to get better so that she could leave.

One day, Kevin visited her and he was crying. Since Andrea had been admitted to hospital, he had asked his sister

Kathleen to take care of Kilo – all his hours visiting Andrea at the hospital plus his working hours meant that he couldn't give the pup the attention he needed and deserved.

Kevin was in such a state that he could barely break the news to Andrea.

'Kathleen has sold Kilo,' he sobbed. 'I don't know where he's gone.'

Kathleen gave no explanation as to why she had decided to sell the dog but Andrea believed that it was because she needed the money.

The news was devastating for Andrea and sent her into another downward spiral. She was plagued with thoughts of her beloved Kilo. Where was he? Were his new owners taking care of him? Was he being abused? Was he missing her? It was too much for her fragile mind. Kevin was heartbroken to see Andrea so upset and promised that he would find Kilo no matter what.

Andrea struggled to get herself back together again, but the thought of finding Kilo spurred her on to get out of the place she called her 'prison'. Before too long, her determination paid off and Andrea was discharged from hospital.

The very day she left the hospital, Andrea and Kevin went to see Kathleen and she demanded to be told where her dog was. It turned out that Kathleen had sold him to a neighbour across the street, so they went and banged on the door.

'You bought my dog off Kathleen,' Andrea said, when the door opened. 'I want him back – he wasn't hers to sell. I know you paid one hundred pounds for him and I'm prepared to pay you that if you let me have him back.'

'You can't have him back,' said the young man. 'He's called Tyson now and I've just sold him. He won't even know you any more.'

Andrea offered him all the money out of her purse, £170, to return the dog. Thankfully he agreed, but they had to wait an agonising night before they were reunited.

As soon as Andrea saw him, she shouted his name and Kilo bounded straight over to her, his face full of joy. He hadn't forgotten his mum in the slightest and he was thrilled to be with her again.

Since then, the pair have been inseparable and Kilo has continued to be a huge influence on Andrea's life. She once smoked fifty cigarettes a day but gave up smoking when the vet said that Kilo needed more exercise and that she needed to get healthier. Andrea lost weight for him and has never been fitter.

'This dog has saved my sanity on more than one occasion,' says Andrea. 'He literally saved my life when I was going to kill myself. If it wasn't for the thought of leaving him alone, I would have gone through with it. I think that somebody sent Kilo to me because he's definitely my little guardian angel. With a history of depression and anxiety, he's been the constant in my life. He's often the only one who can cheer me up – I look into those beautiful, faithful eyes and I can't be sad any more. We sit on the sofa together and he puts a protective paw on my knee, as if to say, *This is my mum –*

she's all mine and I love her. I couldn't be without him. He's more than a pet – he's a lifeline.'

Not content with improving the life of one human being, Kilo has also played an incredible role with Kevin's daughter Natalie.

Coincidentally, Natalie suffered from mental health problems during her adolescence. When she was 17 years old and living with a friend while she finished school, she fell into a depression that escalated quickly. By the time she was 18, Natalie had reached a new low.

Andrea was a rock to her stepdaughter because she understood what she was going through, but Natalie also had another supporter – Kilo.

'One night, I was self-harming,' says Natalie. 'I don't know where my head was that night. I was at a friend's house and I cut my left arm so badly that I was bleeding everywhere. It was a cry for help. My friend came home and she took me to the hospital, where I was sectioned because I had suicidal thoughts. I still don't know what I was sad about, but whatever it was I couldn't just snap out of it. It was deep-rooted and I wanted to die. I was in the hospital

He's more than a pet – he's a lifeline

for ten days and it was the worst time of my life. I was given medication and counselling, and I vowed to get out of there. I hated the feeling that I was being held against my will. It was a huge motivator for me getting out of there.'

When Natalie came out of hospital and went back to live with her dad and Andrea, who had reunited, she struggled to sleep. When everyone went to bed at night, Kilo would stay with her and his presence was a huge comfort to Natalie. Kilo seemed to know that Natalie was suffering and he wanted to help. Just as with Andrea, Kilo followed Natalie around as if he was keeping close tabs on her. When she felt like crying, he was there to mop up her tears.

'Kilo made me feel safe,' says Natalie. 'Even though he and Andrea were inseparable, he took a huge interest in me and what I was going through, like he knew I was struggling and I needed a friend. I had support from human friends but, honestly, he was the best therapy for me. In the still of the night, I would talk to him and tell him my deepest, darkest thoughts and he would just be there, ever present, with a kiss to tell me everything was going to be OK. He didn't judge me. I wasn't afraid that he would abandon me because of my health problems. He didn't need to understand what I was going through – he just had to be there for me, and that he definitely was.

I wouldn't have recovered without that sweet boy. We would go out for walks, just the two of us, and he would never be far from me, like he was always protecting me and watching out for me. Kilo was a very special friend.'

It was through Kilo that Natalie developed a keen interest in rescue dogs. She knew that one day, when she fell in love and had a place of her own, she wanted her own pet to support her through life's trials and tribulations.

In May 2015, Natalie and her partner Emma were on a two-week holiday in Turkey, when they came across a poor dog, an English Pointer, lying in a street in Marmaris. The mutt was in terrible shape and was so sick that they thought he must be dying. The stray was very thin and refused the food they offered him; Emma went into the nearest McDonald's and bought him a cheeseburger and got him a cup of water, but he refused to touch either.

Knowing that the dog would soon be dead unless they intervened, Natalie cornered the animal and used her belt as a leash to catch him. The pair hailed a taxi and took him to the nearest veterinary clinic for help. The once beautiful animal was seriously ill because of a huge gash that went right across his side. It had become infected and the vet said that if it wasn't for Emma and Natalie, he would have died a slow, painful death.

The girls spent the rest of their holiday visiting the dog at the vet, taking him sausages and bacon from their hotel breakfasts. Even though he was very timid initially, he started to come out of his shell for them. They decided to name him Duke.

Natalie and Emma knew that they couldn't leave him – if they did, he would probably be thrown back onto the streets to a certain death. When they returned home to Rotherham, they started a fundraising campaign to bring him to the UK to start a new life. Meanwhile, they paid £100 to send him to a lady in Turkey who could take care of him, ensuring he had the necessary injections and care, thus enabling him to be transported to the UK.

It took them five months to get Duke to the UK, but a local newspaper caught wind of their story and the pair were inundated by kind-hearted animal lovers, who donated the rest of the money for Duke to be driven to the UK in an air-conditioned van.

Now the girls are fundraising to rehome another Turkish street dog in England, so she can start a safe new life in her own *fur*ever home.

'We live with four rescue dogs,' says Natalie. 'They are our world and there's nothing we wouldn't do for them. They give us so much love and attention, and they are always there no matter what. They always cheer me up if I'm having a down day. Kilo was such a support for me during one of the most difficult periods of my life. Despite the fact that he had been abused when he was a puppy, he had so much love and hope to give me and Andrea. His difficult start didn't stop him from being the biggest support and comfort we could ever have known. We still share a unique bond, even though I don't live at home any more. I'm so thankful he has such a big heart. He's eleven years old now and he's tired, but he always has the time to make me and Andrea feel special and loved. Kilo is our rock and he always will be.'

CHAPTER 15

JUSTIN AND BELLA'S STORY

In spring 2012, Justin and his wife Rachel were browsing through Craig's List, a website through which people sell just about anything, when they spotted an advert for a dog. They had an eight-year-old dog called Lucky, a white Westie (West Highland White), and they were looking for a companion for her. The advert said that a driver had found a dog wandering the streets near the couple's home town of El Paso in Texas and that she needed a permanent home because her rescuer already had three dogs of his own. If no one adopted her from Craig's List, then she would have to be taken to the local dog shelter. Justin and Rachel knew that most of the dog shelters in their area were kill shelters (these shelters only keep rescued dogs for a few days or a week, and if they're not adopted during this time then they are killed), so they decided to take Lucky along to meet the dog.

A beautiful brindle hound–retriever mix, she was very thin and malnourished but otherwise seemed healthy enough and she was very friendly towards Lucky. They took her home and she slotted in well with the entire family, although she made it clear right from the start that Justin was her human. She loved Rachel too but it was Justin who she followed around and whose lap she would claim on the sofa.

The worst part of Justin's job as a military logistics expert was being stationed thousands of miles away from Rachel, and they found it particularly tough when Rachel fell pregnant with their first child. Soon after they found out they were expecting, in February 2013, Justin was stationed with his crew in Qatar. While Justin was posted overseas, he was glad to have Bella at home to protect Rachel. She was a dog with a loud bark and he knew that she would instinctively go for someone who broke in, so she was security for when Justin couldn't be there.

Early on in the pregnancy, Rachel suffered a massive bleed and was told by doctors that she had placenta praevia, where her low-lying placenta partially covered her cervix. This meant that she was a high-risk pregnancy and she had to go to the hospital every other week for a check-up. Rachel aimed to keep positive that everything would work out, and she would talk to Justin up to five times a day on FaceTime to assure him that she and their unborn child were doing well.

'We were lucky because we could talk regularly throughout the day, so me being so far away could have been a lot worse,' says Justin. 'It was disappointing because, of course, I wanted to be with Rachel every step of her pregnancy. I wanted to see our first child growing inside her belly and to be there at every hospital appointment to hold Rachel's hand. I missed it all, which as a husband was devastating. We had to get on with it because, being in the army, I didn't have a choice, so FaceTiming each other was very important. Seeing and talking to Rachel gave me peace of mind when I was so far away.'

Rachel's pregnancy progressed well until one evening close to her due date. It was just after 7 p.m. and she and Justin were already FaceTiming as she walked through the door of their home after work. Everywhere was in darkness, so she picked her way down the hall to put the light on. Justin missed Bella too while he was away so he was always excited to see her on his phone. Rachel walked towards the kitchen, where Bella was in her cage, when a man wearing a ski mask suddenly appeared behind her.

Justin saw him first and he asked Rachel who it was. As Rachel turned around, the man stabbed her ferociously in her neck, her breast, her face and in the bone above her left eye. Justin was on the other end of the phone, powerless as he saw the knife plunging into his wife and heard every sickening scream.

'It all happened quickly and all I could see was the shadow of the intruder,' recalls Justin. 'Rachel started to scream it was our friend Corey, and as he stabbed her the phone flew from her hand to the ground. I could hear everything as he attacked my wife. He stabbed her nose so hard that he shattered it. He stabbed the outside of her right eye and down the back of her neck that caused damage to her spine. Rachel fought back as much as she could but she was powerless. He grabbed her left arm and snapped it like it was a twig and then it all went quiet. I didn't know it at the time but Rachel, who was terrified he might stab her stomach and hurt our child, lay down and pretended to be dead. She told me later that it seemed like an eternity until Corey ran out of the house. All the time I was going out of my mind because I wasn't there and I couldn't do anything to save my wife. For all I knew, she was dead.'

Earlier that day, a neighbour had called Rachel at work to say that she thought she had seen someone snooping around her house. Rachel dismissed the person as family friend Corey Moss, who was due to stop by that day to give her money towards the repairs on her car, which he had damaged when he borrowed it. The couple never imagined that he was capable of such heinous actions.

As soon as Corey fled, Rachel dragged her bloodied body across the floor to get her mobile phone. She was paralysed down her right side, so she could barely move but she made it and she called the police, who arrived in minutes.

As they arrived, Justin, who had been frantically trying to call her back, got through and a police officer answered the phone. He

Rachel lay down and pretended to be dead

described the details he'd witnessed of his wife's assault to the police. Rachel was rushed to the local hospital, the University Medical Center in El Paso, where she was immediately taken into surgery to repair her badly broken arm and to have pins and a plate put in it.

Meanwhile Justin started the long journey back to the USA. As he was travelling, Rachel's doctors begged her to deliver the baby, who was starting to become distressed. She refused because she wanted Justin to be there to see the birth and to ensure that if anything happened to her, their baby's loving father would be there to take over.

The next day, 1 November, they started wheeling Rachel down to the theatre for her Caesarean section because they couldn't wait any longer. By a miracle, Justin walked through the doors and was just in time to see Isabella being born. Thankfully, she was an absolutely perfect and healthy newborn baby.

Rachel was in hospital for several weeks, in constant physical and emotional pain. She underwent intensive physical therapy because of the damage to her spine and to the rest of her body where her nerves were damaged from the knife wounds. Rachel was registered blind in one eye and still has part of the knife embedded in her skull; it's too dangerous for doctors to operate so she has to cope with headaches that serve as a constant reminder of the worst day of her life. She is also registered disabled and has to walk with a cane.

The first few months of Isy's life were incredibly hard for Rachel and Justin. Rachel was limited as to how much she could do for her baby while her wounds healed, and the persistent pain made her depressed and withdrawn. Justin took time off work to help out with the baby and, although he kept a brave face for Rachel and Isy's sakes, on the inside he was facing his own demons as he struggled to come to terms with what had happened.

'I had severe stress and anxiety,' says Justin. 'I was so angry that Corey Moss, someone who we had opened our home to and made our friend, tried to kill Rachel and my baby. I wanted to hurt him like he had hurt us. I also felt incredibly guilty that I wasn't home to protect my family. I know that it wasn't my fault because of the job, but that didn't help. I couldn't help thinking that if I'd been there, he wouldn't have tried to attack Rachel and we wouldn't have found ourselves in such a terrible place. I had very dark thoughts all of the time. I tried to be there to support Rachel because she was having such horrendous health problems but inside I was so damaged. Seeing and hearing someone attack the person you love isn't something you can come to terms with quickly. I couldn't get her screams out of my head.'

There was no trial because, in September 2014, Corey Moss pleaded guilty to burglary of habitation with intent to commit a felony and was given a 30-year sentence.

Justin took months off from the army in order to drive Rachel to her many hospital appointments and to help take care of Isy. What should have been a happy time for the couple, celebrating the birth of their much-wanted first child together, was anything but.

Throughout the whole ordeal, the one constant in their lives has been their loyal dog Bella. She has done more for Justin than his doctors and antidepressants ever have.

On the day that Rachel was attacked, Bella was going frantic in her cage in the kitchen – Rachel always put her in the cage when she was out at work, as Bella had grown up this way and felt safer there while her owners were out – so she witnessed the whole terrifying incident and, like Justin, she was unable to help.

'When Rachel would FaceTime when I was overseas, Bella would hear my voice and she would push her face to the phone so that she could see me,' recalls Justin. 'I would talk to her and she would respond with excited little yelps as if she was telling me about her day. It was so funny and it was a comfort for me knowing that she was there for Rachel when I wasn't. When I got home after Rachel was attacked, Bella had to be in a shelter for a few days until we got home. As soon as she heard my voice I could tell that she had missed me because she was crying loudly. I believe that she was also traumatised because she had seen everything.

'When we got home she scoured the whole house as if she was checking to make sure there was no one there. I feel like she would have been going crazy not being able to help Rachel and it preyed on her mind, just like it did mine.'

Since the unthinkable event, Justin has changed and Rachel admits that he's not the same happy-go-lucky man she married. He's prone to violent outbursts due to his anxiety and he's been known to stay in bed for days on end, alone with his thoughts about being powerless to protect his wife. Justin isn't one to cry about his life. Instead he shows his anxiety in the form of hostility towards family and friends. He's continually working to get it under control but it's been an ongoing struggle – and it's Bella who has brought him back from the brink every time.

Once, he was so angry that he punched a laptop and smashed it into a wall. Another time he picked up their king-size bed and threw it across the room. There was also an incident when he threw the fridge into the kitchen wall. Each time, it was Bella who tried to stop him.

'She would cry around me and try to put her head in my hand as if she was reminding me to stay calm,' says Justin. 'On these occasions, I did eventually stop and come to my senses when she wouldn't leave me alone. Things could have got so much more out of control if she hadn't been brave enough to get involved. Now when she senses I'm becoming hostile or aggravated, she tries to calm me down before I can't stop myself. Bella will try to sit on my knee or nuzzle my legs or hands to remind me that she's there. Often seeing her there is enough for me to pull myself together and avert a situation. Even in bed she lies with me and she relaxes me – it's amazing.'

Bella doesn't allow Justin to be by himself, so she follows him into the bathroom, the bedroom, the lounge... She has also become extra protective of Rachel, Isy and their new baby, also called Justin, who was born in November 2015. Wherever any of them are in the house, so is Bella, ready to protect and serve.

If it wasn't for Bella, life would be even more stressful and difficult. This rescue dog has immersed herself into her adopted family more than they could ever have hoped.

'Bella is definitely my security system,' says Justin. 'She stops me from getting out of control when I'm feeling hostile. While I would never hurt my family, the anger that I feel because this happened to us does reach crisis levels. Thankfully Bella is there to defuse most situations.

'She rescues me every single day from myself. I honestly don't know what I would do without her. I know we saved her from a possible death at the shelter but she continues to repay us every single day. Bella is an extension of our family and we love her more than anything.'

she continues to repay
us every single day

CHAPTER 16

JOSIE AND NOEL'S STORY

When she was put into foster care as a young girl, Josie had already endured more emotional upheaval than many people do in a lifetime. Her home life had been very dysfunctional because she had never known who – if anyone – would be at home to care for her. More often than not, her mother acted as a single parent, but she couldn't give Josie the proper care and attention she deserved. A victim of severe neglect, Josie was regularly left without parental supervision, and without regular meals or bedtimes. When the foster care system intervened, Josie was eight and her father was nowhere to be seen.

Josie was placed with her new foster family in Wales: Jennifer and her husband John. The couple had decided to become foster carers when Jennifer wasn't able to fall pregnant; she had almost died from a brain haemorrhage when she was 40, and they had stopped trying for a baby of their own, thinking that perhaps this just wasn't meant to be.

'My brain haemorrhage was a real wake-up call for us both,' says Jennifer. 'I was lucky to be alive and we realised that we had to start living our lives to the full rather than dwelling on something that wasn't happening for us. John is wonderful with children and we live on a remote farm in the countryside with miles of acreage, so we felt that we had an awful lot to offer to a child in the foster care system. We knew it wasn't going to be easy but, if anything, knowing this spurred us on to help. We had several teenagers who came to live with us and then, in 2011, Josie came to stay. From the moment she arrived, my heart broke because she was so damaged. She didn't know what love meant.'

Josie was extremely anxious and clung to Jennifer, especially if meeting new people or going somewhere for the first time. Jennifer immediately established a set routine, so Josie knew exactly when she was getting up in the morning, going to bed and eating her meals. This regular, daily pattern helped her to start adjusting. Once, Josie went on a school trip with the other children from her class, but Jennifer only managed to persuade her to attend by getting her to take Jennifer's teddy bear with her as a token of reassurance since that helped her to understand that she would be going home that night to return it to her guardian. Josie found it difficult to communicate her feelings; her frustration led to screaming fits and tantrums then tears that could last for days.

'Josie was prone to going off the rails if something reminded her of the past, or if somebody said anything that she didn't like,' recalls Jennifer. 'It was as if she couldn't be reminded of the life she had before us because it was too painful. Sometimes she would cry for hours on my shoulder and I would hold her tight to show her that we're never going to leave her. Other times, her sorrow would manifest itself as bad behaviour and tantrums at school and at home. This was very difficult to deal with, particularly all the answering back to me and John. I had to learn to walk away for all of our sakes, until she calmed down and got all the anguish and anger out of her system.'

For months Jennifer felt that they were walking on eggshells, trying to avoid scenarios that might anger or sadden Josie. She needed constant reassurance that, unlike her real parents, Jennifer and John weren't going to abandon her. Josie agreed to stay with Jennifer and John permanently, already calling Jennifer Mum, but she became increasingly withdrawn as her anxiety resurfaced. This time, nothing Jennifer said or did could entice Josie out of her shell.

Josie turned a corner in December 2013, and it was all thanks to the cutest puppy that Jennifer had ever seen. A lifelong animal lover, Jennifer owns several horses and adopted dogs, and helps to walk dogs at the local dog rescue shelter in her spare time; being around the animals gives her a sense of peace and happiness. This particular day, just before Christmas, a dog was in the grooming room being bathed and having its fur clipped ready to be advertised for adoption. The dog had been roaming the streets on a council estate and had been taken by a dog warden to the shelter to be assessed.

The dog was a thin, dirty, stinking, matted hairball. The kennel staff had thought it must be a bitch since the animal always squatted to take a pee. After a bath it was revealed that 'she' was in fact a male dog; he had been so weighed down with masses of fur that he hadn't been able to cock his leg to take a pee like a male dog usually would. The vet thought he was probably a Yorkshire Terrier crossed with a Shih Tzu, aged approximately one year, and he was small, weighing in at only 1.2 kg. The kneecaps in his back legs kept on slipping, indicating that he had spent considerable time cooped up in a small cage.

As the black-and-brown terrier with the long, fluffy tail stood on the grooming table, shivering uncontrollably because there was no heating in the kennels, Jennifer's heart melted and she suddenly had an idea. Jennifer got in her car and raced back to their house, four miles away, where Josie was doing her homework.

'Put your coat on and come with me,' she said to a surprised Josie. 'I've got something to show you.'

Josie still didn't know what was going on when they arrived at the shelter.

'What do you think, Josie?' asked Jennifer as they walked to his kennel. 'Look at him – he's yours!'

The terrier was dry but still shivering, his black eyes gleaming with interest at his new surroundings.

Josie looked at Jennifer, her eyes huge with surprise, and Jennifer nodded.

'Give your new friend a hug!' Jennifer said. 'Go on – he needs a good hug and some loving.'

With tears rolling down both their faces, Josie cradled her new dog, who nestled his small face into the crook of her arm as if he'd been there all his life. It was an intensely emotional moment for Josie and Jennifer, who instinctively knew that she had done the right thing for her foster daughter. The way the girl and the dog connected was incredible to witness. All the way home in the back of the car, Josie held the dog, whom she named Noel, wrapped in a blanket to keep him warm. Noel kept looking at her for reassurance, licking her fingers and her face as if to make sure that she was real.

The next few days were a blur of activity. Noel was diagnosed with kennel cough and Josie administered special medicine every few hours. Jennifer bought him a sweater to keep him warm as his coat had been clipped short, while Josie rubbed menthol onto his chest to help him breathe more easily.

They tried keeping Noel in a large cage in the kitchen at night, but he found a way to escape the confines of his cage or he would bark at the top of his lungs to wake everyone up. The family soon accepted that Noel always found his way upstairs to Josie's room, where she snuggled him into bed with her. Jennifer could already

 Josie cradled her new dog, who nestled his small face into the crook of her arm as if he'd been there all his life

see Noel's effect on Josie and was more than happy with the arrangement because it alleviated Josie's fear of being alone at night.

'It was as if they were meant to find each other,' says Jennifer. 'Noel was the sweetest little dog imaginable and it was clear from the start that he regarded Josie as "his" human. Josie really took his care to heart. Nothing was too much trouble and I think he gave her a sense of self-worth for the first time in her life. She had to be strong and responsible for him because Noel was her charge and she was the one who walked and fed him. I witnessed a change in Josie after Noel arrived and it was definitely a change for the better.'

After Noel's appearance, Josie's anxiety attacks and angry outbursts became far less frequent. If she's anxious, the first thing she reaches for is Noel; she takes him to her room and tells him how she's feeling, knowing he won't judge her. Noel is Josie's shoulder to cry on; he instinctively knows when she's having a hard time and it's amazing what a lick on her face or a cuddle from her dog can do for her. Not only is Josie a much calmer young woman now that she has Noel, but he has also taught her life lessons in trust. Her pet is a constant in her world and she knows that, no matter what, he loves her unconditionally – because that's what dogs do when they find someone they truly connect with.

While Josie is a long-term member of the family, Jennifer still fosters other children from time to time and every single one has fallen for the little dog with the cheeky personality.

'Noel is an icebreaker when I have new children come to stay,' says Jennifer. 'He's very cute and kind and they love to pet him. He absolutely laps up all the attention. I tell the children that Noel didn't have a very nice life but now he's happy since he came to live with us. I draw a parallel between the kids and the dog so that they can see that one day they'll have the nice life they dreamed about too – it *is* within their reach. Josie is happy to share him with anyone. She understands how this little dog has helped her and she appreciates his love more than anything in the world. He keeps her calm on a horrible day and he's the only one who can bring her smile back when she's feeling upset. Noel is her rock.'

Jennifer also owns Ben, a brindle Lurcher that she adopted from a kennel ten years ago, and Noel and Ben have become firm friends. Ben had been abandoned by travellers on a local street and was in a terrible state as he had been run over by a car and was suffering from mange.

'It's as if Ben and Noel realise that they come from similar backgrounds,' says Jennifer. 'They're like partners in crime, always there for each other, always running around chasing each other. I think that Josie is Noel's best human friend and Ben is his closest doggy pal. He's such a huge part of both their lives that neither of them could do without him. Noel is a blessing and I'm so thankful that we have him. It's amazing how this one little ball of silky smooth fur has made such a difference to Josie's life. He turned her into a kinder, more caring person. When she needs him most, he's always there – Josie's knight in shining armour. Well, her saviour in a pullover!'

CHAPTER 17

MICHELLE AND PANCHO'S STORY

When Michelle rescued her first dog, Jinny, she had struggled through several years of emotional trauma. It quickly became clear after they got married that Michelle and her husband Paul were having problems conceiving, which led to years of IVF cycles and hormones, disappointment and frustration.

When Michelle turned 27 years old, she miraculously fell pregnant. She couldn't believe their good fortune after everything they had been through. However, it turned out to be a rare ectopic pregnancy where the baby was forming in her Fallopian tube. After being told that she had suffered a miscarriage, Michelle was rushed into surgery to remove the ruptured tube.

'I was numb and devastated when it happened,' recalls Michelle. 'All my hopes and dreams for my baby were gone. I was lucky that it was found before it completely ruptured because then I could have died. After the ectopic pregnancy,

I was severely traumatised and shocked, so much so that my doctor likened my feelings to post-traumatic stress disorder and I had to stop working. I had flashbacks of losing the baby all the time. I couldn't sit still and read a book or watch the TV because I couldn't get it out of my head. I couldn't ever relax – I had no peace. I was going out of my mind living in a world where I was reliving what happened over and over.'

Paul suggested that they get a rescue dog to keep Michelle company when he was at work. Michelle had always worked hard and Paul thought a dog might give her a different focus.

When they scoured the local rescue centres in Yorkshire, they found Jinny, a German Shepherd–collie cross who was ten months old. She was a cute, gangly bundle of brown fur who had been dumped at the kennel twice before when people had adopted her but then regretted it.

Jinny certainly had emotional issues. For starters, she was very nervous around people – apart from Michelle and Paul. For the first three days, she clung to Michelle and wouldn't get off her knee, but she was always nervous around other people, particularly men. While it was comforting that Jinny had made such a great connection with Michelle, this led to new problems as the puppy suffered from severe separation anxiety. When Michelle and Paul went out and left her alone in the house, Jinny would be incredibly destructive in their absence. Once, she tore a new carpet – it had only been fitted the day before – to shreds all the way down an entire staircase. She chewed table legs, chairs and a sofa, so her new owners could see why she may have been returned to the shelter twice already.

Yet Michelle loved her from the start and, instead of taking the easy way out by returning her to the shelter, she invested a lot of time in training her properly. They spent hours together while Michelle trained Jinny to sit and stay, to come to her while off the lead, and to walk by her side when they were out at the park. Jinny was a challenge, but she couldn't have entered Michelle's life at a better time.

'We shared a special bond,' recalls Michelle. 'Jinny became my soulmate. She followed me everywhere; she was my shadow so I was never alone when Paul wasn't home. Training her took up so much time but, while I was working with her, I wasn't sitting on my own brooding about losing my baby or dwelling on my infertility problems. I was focused on her and it was good for my mindset. And while her separation anxiety eased, so did my anxiety. Being with Jinny made me calm and even though I still had bad days, they were fewer and further between with Jinny to hold my hand.'

The couple soon adopted another rescue dog as a companion for Jinny, a collie–Labrador cross called Dougal, who quickly became a valued family member.

When Michelle's dad, Derek, died after a short battle with kidney cancer, Jinny was there for Michelle. Not long after Derek passed away, Paul moved to a new job in Shropshire. It was a great position but bad timing as Michelle couldn't move and leave her mum just yet, so Paul stayed there during the week and returned home at weekends.

Michelle suffered another miscarriage, this time at ten weeks, and it was Jinny who pulled her owner through when she felt as if her heart was breaking at the loss of another much-wanted baby.

Almost 18 months after her dad died, Michelle moved to be with Paul in Shropshire. Their house was in the country, so they had few neighbours. Making friends was an uphill struggle and Michelle felt lonely.

'Leaving Mum in Yorkshire was very hard for me,' says Michelle. 'She didn't have Dad any more and I worried about her all the time, even though she would visit me often. I found making friends very difficult. If I'd had kids, I think it would have been easier to meet other mums at the school gates, or at the kids' clubs or at birthday parties. When you're childless, it's not easy meeting new people. Thankfully, though, I had Jinny, who was my constant companion. If it wasn't for her I wouldn't have made the transition at all. I'd have run back to Yorkshire.'

Two years after the move, Jinny started falling over and bumping into furniture as if she had lost control of her legs. The vet's diagnosis was stark. Jinny had suffered a stroke and was probably dying before their eyes.

For six long months, Michelle witnessed the decline of her best friend but she refused to give up on her. Jinny became incontinent, which distressed her, and Michelle would get up three or four times in the night to clean her up. Jinny would stare at Michelle as if she was pleading with her for help, as if she didn't want to die and leave her beloved humans. In the end, Michelle had to make the decision to have Jinny put to sleep. She had wished for so long that the beautiful soul would pass away peacefully in her sleep, but it didn't happen that way.

Not long after Jinny's passing, Dougal became ill and Michelle realised just how much Jinny had been there for him, too. Dougal was blind and deaf, and he seemed more clumsy without Jinny. It became clear that Jinny had been leading her friend around the house; she had been his eyes and ears. Dougal was mourning her too. Soon after Jinny was put down, Dougal passed away from cancer and diabetes, which left Michelle newly heartbroken.

'I told Paul: no more dogs,' says Michelle. 'I couldn't cope with watching another dog die, with having to make the decision to put them to sleep when the time came. I couldn't think about the anxiety it caused when they were ill, or the sense of deep loss I felt when they had gone. It was as traumatic in some ways as losing my dad because those dogs were my family too. When they died, I felt as if my heart had been ripped out.'

At the age of 43, Michelle was rushed into hospital with another ectopic pregnancy. She became so upset that she was put on antidepressants to help her get through her days.

For weeks afterwards, Michelle was so desperately sad all the time that she couldn't function. Her anxiety peaked again and, in desperation because she hated being in the house alone, she went back to work too soon and against her doctors' advice.

Paul knew that Michelle needed a four-legged friend and suggested another dog to bring some much-needed life back into their empty home. As Michelle trawled dog adoption websites, she realised that she should have got a dog after Jinny and Dougal died – perhaps then she would have coped better with the latest ectopic pregnancy.

There were so many homeless dogs that picking only one was a difficult task, until a shelter emailed a photograph of a tiny, fluffy black puppy to Michelle's inbox. The forlorn pup was four months old but looked as though he bore the weight of the world on his shoulders. Until his rescue he had been living in an allotment shed. Michelle was excited about this dog but there was one slight hitch – he was in Spain.

'I didn't know how this could work,' says Michelle. 'I phoned the lady at the rescue centre and she explained that she worked to help a tiny organisation called TIKA run by two amazing British ladies (TIna and KAren) living in Spain. These two ladies dedicate their lives to rescuing and rehoming stray and abandoned dogs, arranging for them to have blood screens and pet passports to enable them to travel to the UK if they're lucky enough to find homes. I knew I was taking a huge leap of faith adopting a dog I'd never even met, but I just had a good feeling about this little dog. His eyes were kind and he was definitely very cute – I couldn't not have him.'

It took a couple of months for the dog, Pancho, to be prepared for the two-day drive from Spain to the UK. When he finally walked into his new home for the first time, it was like a whirlwind of energy hit Michelle. He was always very sociable and headstrong – just the remedy to drag Michelle back from her black moods. He gave her something to get up for in the morning and he rekindled a spark in Michelle that had been missing since Jinny and Dougal.

Pancho has completely changed Michelle's life since even before he arrived. While she was waiting for him to be driven to the UK from Spain, she set up her first Facebook account where she could follow the progress of his journey. This meant that she met other people who were waiting for their dogs to arrive and this in turn led her to Spanish Stray Dogs UK, through which she later found Alfie, a Spanish hunting dog, and Pol, a stray she originally fostered but fell so in love with that she had to keep him. As Michelle says, she would never have got so involved with the charity and she would never have made so many new friends had she not signed up for social media to track Pancho's journey. She has travelled all over the country and to Spain with the charity, meeting new people. She says: 'I always say that Pancho really did give me the world. He opened up my eyes to a life beyond the four walls of my house where I was keeping myself almost hidden from the rest of my life. I have a real purpose now, thanks to

*He ignited the spark
back into my soul*

Pancho, and for the first time in years it is something I feel passionate about. He ignited the spark back into my soul and he changed my perspective for the better.'

Michelle is now actively involved with Spanish Stray Dogs UK, where she works on campaigns with a small team of dedicated volunteers to raise funds to feed, care for and find loving homes for over three hundred abandoned and stray dogs in a municipal shelter in southern Spain. She travels throughout the UK to help connect prospective owners with the dogs. She also meets other owners throughout the country who have adopted Spanish dogs and provides help and advice to anyone considering this option. Michelle has so many like-minded friends who care about her that she is never lonely. Pancho, Alfie and Pol have brought so much positivity and so many new people into her life that she will be forever thankful to them.

'My rescue dogs have always been my child substitutes,' Michelle says, smiling. 'I've always loved animals, so my dogs naturally became second best to having a child and they have always been a huge comfort to me. They have been my light at the end of a horrible day. Just by having them in a room makes me feel calmer and much happier. They have been my greatest friends during the most difficult times of my life. They have proved to be more than family – they are my everything.'

CHAPTER 18

ANGELA AND LIAM'S STORY

Saviours come in all shapes and sizes – Angela's saviour just happened to be a curly-haired dog with a limp, who did more to make her happy than she could possibly have imagined after she rescued him from an animal shelter.

Angela had suffered from anxiety throughout her teenage years. It was so severe that even watching a harrowing story on the news worried her so much that she would be nervous for days, terrified that the same thing might happen to her. When Angela left school to go to the University of North Dakota, an hour from home, her symptoms gradually became worse. Away from the security of her loving family and the safety of her home, she found it increasingly difficult to cope.

She would wake up in the morning with her stomach bloated and in painful knots. As soon as she got up, she would worry about being late for her class, about handing her university coursework in on time and about getting to the gym to do her daily workout.

As Angela's anxiety took hold of her, she felt that the only thing in her life that she could control were her eating habits. She would weigh herself upwards of five or six times a day to ensure she didn't put on weight; if she was a few pounds heavier, she would eat less or work out more to compensate. Angela didn't eat three meals per day; instead she ate small, calorie-controlled portions every few hours that would be planned according to her recent weight reading. She cut out all proteins and existed on only fruit, vegetables and rice crackers.

It was a miserable existence. She was constantly tired because she was eating fewer than a thousand calories per day which isn't nearly enough for a grown woman who was studying for long hours and exercising every day. Even though she was exhausted, Angela never missed a gym session because, in her mind, it helped to keep her weight down and cancelled out all the calories she had eaten that day.

In some ways, strict control over her eating habits helped to ease her anxiety, but it certainly wasn't healthy or safe.

She lost most of her friends because she never went out or made an effort to socialise; she simply came home from university, slept and watched TV. Angela was secretive about her eating problems, so her housemate Reeca didn't notice that anything was wrong, and at the time Angela didn't think she had a problem as such. That is, until she went out for dinner with her parents, Lori and Rick, and her brother, Eric.

She was home for the weekend and they decided to go to a local Italian restaurant famous for its delicious, fattening pasta sauces. While everyone else enjoyed the menu on offer, Angela ordered only a bowl of broth.

'I wasn't even eating it; I was just playing with it,' recalls Angela. 'Mum noticed what I was doing and she asked me about my anxiety. That's when it all came out and I told them that I thought I had a problem with food. I finally realised that my eating habits weren't normal and it was terrifying. My anxiety peaked and I dropped out of college to come home and get help.'

 I couldn't see a light at the end of the tunnel

In spring 2012, Angela was tested and assessed at the Sanford Eating Disorders and Weight Management Center in Fargo. She was diagnosed with an Eating Disorder Not Otherwise Specified (EDNOS). At 5 ft 11 in. and 10 stone, she was definitely too skinny, and her doctors warned that, if she didn't seek help, it was only a matter of time before she would become anorexic.

Angela went through a lot of counselling and, gradually, she was encouraged to eat proper meals, which took a lot of getting used to after skipping them for so long. It was a tough time, and there were moments when Angela felt like she would never get better and the life she so desperately wanted seemed so far away that it was impossible to imagine.

'I remember breaking down and crying on Mum's shoulder many times,' says Angela. 'I couldn't see a light at the end of the tunnel. I was supposed to be eating more but I couldn't face it, even though I knew that I had to do it to get better. I locked myself away from the world. It was easier not to see my friends and to have to explain what was going on, so I locked myself in the basement and watched TV or slept. It was a lonely existence and I couldn't see a way out. I was trapped and I didn't know what to do. The anxiety and the unhappiness ruled my life for a long time. There were good days but there were a whole lot more bad days. I struggled and I didn't know when or how it would end. It was an awful life. I was just so unhappy and I felt worthless because I was making a mess out of everything.'

Angela felt so lonely that she talked to her parents about getting a dog. She thought that an older dog would be best so she didn't have to train it while she was still recovering from her eating disorder. Rick, her dad, is allergic to dogs so the family had never had one in the house before, but Angela did some research into hypoallergenic dogs. Rick told her that if she thought it would help her and if she could find a hypoallergenic dog, he would consider adopting a dog. Angela scoured the local rescue centres and, incredibly, it didn't take her long to find one: a beautiful snowy-white Lhasa Apso–poodle mix.

The four-year-old dog had been found on the streets, and he was so dirty it was assumed that he had been living on his own for a while. When Liam was brought to the Fargo-Moorhead Humane Society shelter, close to Angela's home, he was black with filth and had cysts up and down his spine. The poor boy needed specialist treatment, which, thankfully, helped him pull through.

He was sweet-natured despite his rough background and, according to his profile, he loved human contact so Angela had high hopes. When they first met, he ignored her when she took him outside the shelter to play, and she wondered whether he was the right dog for her. The shelter staff asked her to give him one more chance and they went back inside, where Liam jumped on Angela's knee and he stayed there for thirty minutes.

'We played and he let me scratch his chin and rub his belly,' recalls Angela. 'He didn't leave my side for so long and I told my mum that he was the one and we had to take him home. I felt like we really bonded during that half hour. The shelter lady told me that although he was otherwise healthy, he had chronic dry eye and he would need medication for the rest of his life. That didn't bother me – I wouldn't have wanted someone not to give me a chance because I have health issues, so I was even more determined to get him. I wanted to care for him in the loving way that my parents cared for me. Dad came to see him the next day and, of course, Liam won him over straight away. Within a week he was living at my house and he was just perfect. From the start, he slept in my room and he definitely attached himself to me. Getting him was the most exciting thing I'd done in such a long time and it felt good to feel so enthusiastic again.'

Liam made all the difference to Angela's life. Just having him with her all the time was a huge comfort, and when she wasn't feeling good about herself, he would make it his business to snuggle up to her on the sofa and make her feel warm and protected.

In winter 2012, Liam started swaggering when he walked, and one day he couldn't get up at all. A vet diagnosed him with deviated spinal discs and warned Angela that her beloved boy may never walk again, which would severely impact on his quality of life.

'It was devastating to hear this,' says Angela. 'Liam had done so much for me already, and I knew that we had to do everything in our power to help him even though it was going to cost a small fortune. We found an animal chiropractor and an acupuncturist and he started having special treatments. Amazingly, it worked and now, although he walks with a limp, he can still move about, which the vets said was nothing short of a miracle.'

Since Liam appeared in her life, everything has turned around for Angela. Before she adopted him, she spent many days working herself up into extreme states of anxiety where she couldn't cope and her deepest worry was that she would end up in hospital. However, as the proud owner of Liam, she eventually went back to school and graduated from the University of North Dakota with honours in early education. Angela now has a job she loves, teaching preschool children from families with lower incomes.

'Liam has always been there for me where my family couldn't,' says Angela. 'My family has been an important part of my recovery but Liam was definitely the one who gave me a huge reason to get myself better. It wasn't just his cuddles that made me relax and feel happier – it was the weird noises he would make that would make me laugh out loud, and the way he would lick the whole of my face, or he would bark loudly at absolutely nothing. On the days when I was tired and I didn't feel like eating, I made myself both sleep and eat because I figured if I was too ill to look after him, it wasn't fair. I had an obligation to him – he didn't ask to be adopted by me and as such I had to take care of him even if I felt lousy. Liam gave me purpose where I had no purpose. For months I felt like I was in a black hole with nowhere to go, then along comes this lovely white dog who is a complete ray of sunshine. There is nothing better for me than a kiss from him when I get home from work.'

Having Liam inspired Angela to adopt another rescue dog from the same shelter. There had been a local case of a woman hoarding dozens of dogs, several of which were taken in by the Fargo-Moorhead shelter for rehoming. One of these dogs in particular caught Angela's eye when she browsed the shelter's website. Tucker was a hypoallergenic Cocker Spaniel–Lhasa cross, sandy coloured with a huge black button nose. He had lived his entire life – two and a half years – cooped up in a tiny cage.

It was clear that Tucker had barely been handled by humans. He cowered when touched and he was so skittish that he wouldn't sit still for a second – no doubt because, for the first time in his life, he could run around and enjoy a precious sense of freedom.

Angela and her family took him in with the aim of fostering him, but she and Liam fell so in love with Tucker that they ended up keeping him.

Tucker certainly proved to be a challenge. Angela had only had him for a week when he slipped his leash during a walk and went missing for 30 days! His disappearance sparked a full-blown media appeal and search, with his picture appearing all over the TV. Tucker was returned safe and sound and is now enjoying the good life with Angela and his adopted big brother Liam.

She wouldn't be without the two rescue dogs who have given so much back to her.

'Liam is a great stress reliever for me,' says Angela. 'I think that we were meant to find each other. We had both been through a lot in our lives and we both knew what tough times are about, so we helped each other to deal with our own issues. I think that rescue dogs are so special. I know that Liam and Tucker are grateful to me for giving them a home because they repay me every day by showing me love, attention and a lot of happiness. We go through life's ups and downs together, and no matter what happens I will always have my two boys to help and support me.'

CHAPTER 19

YVONNE AND MOLLY'S STORY

A lifelong animal fan, Yvonne had always loved dogs and cats. In December 2012, she travelled to Thailand for almost a month's holiday with her partner Chris and the pair volunteered for a week at the Lanta Animal Welfare charity in Krabi. This small-scale organisation rescues street dogs and cats, patches them up if they are injured or sick, and adopts them out to families all over the world. Yvonne loved walking the dogs along the beach in the early morning sunshine and feeding the hungry residents in the evening. She found it heartbreaking to see all the neglected and abused animals, some in pain from being beaten, others so badly starved that their bones showed through their bodies. But Yvonne realised that this was a place of great hope and that she was helping make a difference, so she embraced her week there and vowed to one day return. It was a humbling experience and she missed the dogs when she left.

When she arrived home in January, her first port of call was her mum and dad, Mary and John, at their Midlands home. Yvonne was very close to them both but particularly to her mother, who was more of a best friend. They had a wonderful weekend catching up and Yvonne told her parents, also huge animal lovers, all about her experience at the dog shelter.

The following Monday morning, Yvonne was in London on business when her father kept calling her. She wasn't allowed to take personal calls at work so had to wait to listen to his frantic voicemail messages. Her dad was crying so much and it sounded as if he said that her old cat Tom had died suddenly – at the time she had two rescue cats who were like family to her and Chris. She was so devastated by the news that she couldn't help crying and she had to leave work.

Half an hour later, after she had pulled herself together, Chris called, sobbing.

'I'm so sorry, Yvonne –' Chris began to say, but Yvonne cut in.

'I know Tom's dead,' she said, and the tears started to flow again. 'I know our boy's gone.'

'Oh my God,' said Chris. 'It's not Tom who died, Yvonne. It's your mum.'

Yvonne's world went black as she collapsed with the shock. How could this be true? She had seen her mum only two days previously and, at 73, she had been as full of life as ever. She had spoken to her mum the evening before and everything had been great. It didn't make any sense that a woman who was never ill could have passed away so suddenly.

Numb with the shock, she went straight to the hospital to be with her dad, who was inconsolable. Her parents had been everything to each other; suddenly, the love of his life was gone. That Monday morning, just as he did every day, John had taken his wife breakfast in bed. She was still sleeping, so rather than disturb her, he went back downstairs to let her rest a little longer.

When she still wasn't up an hour later, he went back upstairs to find she had passed away. Otherwise fit and healthy, her heart had stopped in her sleep and she had died alone.

Yvonne's world ground to a halt after her mum died. Unable to cope with her sudden loss, she was prescribed medication to alleviate the grief and depression. She didn't continue her work as a freelance events manager for months because she had no motivation to find work. She spent all day on the sofa, crying or sleeping, but her sleepless nights were the worst as she would only get an hour or two of rest before she woke up, still upset. To numb her grief, Yvonne got into the habit of drinking two bottles of red wine every night; it seemed to be her only source of comfort.

'My mum's death was so sudden that there was no way anyone could have prepared for it,' says Yvonne. 'I think that's why it hit me so hard. If she'd been ill, maybe it would have been easier to accept but one minute she was alive, the next she was gone. It was so unfair. I also felt tremendous guilt with her passing. I wished that I hadn't spent that Christmas thousands of miles away in Thailand and that I'd spent it with them so that I'd had more time with Mum. I wrestled with all sorts of regrets, it was no wonder I was depressed. I could barely function and Chris was so worried about me. He was my rock at a time when I didn't care whether I lived or died because I'd hit such a low.'

In the early hours of a December morning in 2014, Yvonne was wide awake, surfing the Internet like she always did when she couldn't sleep. Chris had suggested that they get another pet to keep her company when he wasn't there so she was looking through animal rescue sites. Yvonne logged into her Facebook account and watched a video on the page of the Soi Dog Foundation, a charity run by a British couple in Phuket, Thailand. Like Lanta, the Soi Dog Foundation rescues and rehabilitates street dogs in order to rehome them.

The video showed a black-and-white, eight-week-old puppy called Mockingjay, who was believed to be a collie cross-breed. It was thought that she had been foraging for food when someone deliberately threw hot oil over her. A lady discovered her suffering in the street, with horrific burns covering her tiny head and front legs, and took her to the Soi Dog Foundation for help. It was touch-and-go whether Mockingjay would survive but she proved to have an unshakeable spirit. With specialist care and attention, she pulled through and started her long road to recovery.

The dog's face and legs were covered in red, crusty scabs from being scalded by hot oil, and her eyes were so pained that it was impossible to look away. As Yvonne read about the abused dog in Thailand, something inside her stirred. For the first time in months, she desperately cared about something and she resolved to adopt the pup.

'She looked so pathetic in her video and she was shaking in pain as she was held for the cameras,' recalls Yvonne. 'This little dog needed a caring, loving home and I knew I could give it to her. For the first time in years, I felt fired up. I watched that video over and over. And I don't know why, I just had to have that dog. There was something hugely appealing about her – maybe it was because she was in such a terrible state. I wanted to help. I woke Chris up at 5 a.m. and I told him that we had to have that dog. I didn't know how we could get her over to the UK and I didn't even know if she was available for adoption. I just felt that I had to do everything in my power to fight for her. Even though this wasn't the normal kind of rescue dog to take in, Chris supported me. I think he saw a glow in my own dull, pained eyes that he hadn't seen in a long time and he knew that this pup would be good for me. I messaged the Soi Dog Foundation right away and they responded quickly to tell me that there were other people interested in her. But I'm very persistent **He saw a glow in my dull, pained eyes that he hadn't seen in a long time** when I want something and I bombarded them with so many messages that in the end, Christy, the head of adoptions, gave her to me. Christy told me that Mockingjay was one of the most inspirational dogs they'd ever taken in. Her injuries were so severe yet she had shown such strength to survive even when she was in severe pain from the burns. I knew that she was the dog for me because I could relate to such deep-rooted pain.'

Once Yvonne had passed the foundation's strict background checks, she paid them £700 to adopt Mockingjay, a fee which covered her spaying, injections, vet bills and the transportation costs to England. It took five months to get everything together. They had to wait for Mockingjay's health to improve before she could fly and also for another five dogs to become ready to be flown overseas as it was only cost-effective for the charity to send six dogs at a time.

Christy sent Yvonne regular photograph updates of her new doggy and, even during the long wait, Yvonne felt a renewed love for her life. The excitement of preparing for a new addition made her realise that she should get herself better for Mockingjay's sake as much as her own.

How could she be a good owner and give the dog everything she needed if she wasn't feeling good herself?

In May 2015, Mockingjay, renamed Molly by Yvonne, boarded a plane with five other hounds to Phuket, Thailand. They flew to the Netherlands, where they caught a ferry for the final part of their long journey to Harwich in Essex.

Yvonne took a month off work to bond with her new girl and to help Molly with the challenge of adjusting to her new life. Molly had never been in a two-storey house before. She chewed carpets to shreds and buried slippers in the garden.

Yvonne's jewellery kept going missing, only some of which was found in the garden where Molly had left it.

Initially, if Yvonne went out and had to leave Molly in the house, she left her in a closed room with her bed and toys because she thought she might feel safer in there. Instead, Molly panicked because she hated being enclosed, so she ripped the carpets and pulled the curtains down in a heap on the floor. It looked like a bomb had gone off when Yvonne returned home an hour later.

Training Molly on the lead was another challenge because she would pull on it and try to drag Yvonne back to the house or would slip her collar and run away. Yvonne took her to puppy classes but Molly hated everything about them, so they stopped these after a few weeks and Yvonne concentrated on training Molly herself.

There were times when, even though she loved her, Yvonne wondered what she had done by adopting a dog from such a difficult background. However, she always knew that she couldn't give up on Molly – she was the reason she got up every day.

Yvonne consulted a dog therapist, who diagnosed Molly with extreme anxiety, which didn't come as a huge surprise given her difficult start in life. With a lot of understanding and patience, the pair worked through everything together, with the satisfying result that Molly now loves being walked twice a day and she adores her home far away from Thailand.

Molly still has issues, such as hating the noise of children and a terror of bikes and pushchairs, which makes going to the park difficult because she wants to slip her collar and run home. She is still emotionally scarred – sometimes during her sleep she cries softly and tries to touch the scars on her face with her paws, as if reliving the horror of being scalded. Molly's rehabilitation is an ongoing process and one which Yvonne is deeply committed to.

She has grown into a striking dog and has won prizes in two beauty contests – not bad for a dog with fading facial scars. Molly is spoiled rotten by her human parents but Yvonne says that the miracle pup saved her, not the other way round.

'I remember looking at her face that night and something clicked in my head,' recalls Yvonne. 'I suddenly realised that even though I was at rock bottom and I wasn't living, just existing, here was someone who was much worse off than me yet she was fighting to survive. As we prepared for her to come to England, I've never felt so optimistic about anything. She gave me a new purpose, a reason to pull myself together, stop drinking and staying up until the early hours of the morning. If she had the strength to live, then so did I. I also

*If she had the strength
to live, then so did I*

realised that my mum would want me to adopt Molly because it was the right thing to do and she would be good for me. My mum wouldn't want me crying all the time. She would expect me to get out there, bring Molly home and enjoy her. Molly and I go to the cemetery every week to visit my mum's grave and it's like she knows. She sits quietly with me as I think about Mum and often I'll have a cry so Molly snuggles into me and I immediately feel better. She gives me hope for my future. I do wonder sometimes whether my mum sent Molly to pull me out of a very bad time in my life because I genuinely believe we were meant to find each other. We both have emotional scars and no matter what, we find comfort just by being together. Molly is my everything and I'll do my best to care for her like she has cared for me since she arrived.'

I do wonder sometimes whether my mum sent Molly to pull me out of a very bad time in my life

CHAPTER 20

KAI AND KIRA'S STORY

The old saying 'mother knows best' definitely rings true in Cat's case because she was always convinced that there was something going on with her baby boy. When her twins, Mari and Kai, were born one month premature, Kai was rushed into the intensive care unit of their local California hospital. He was a little floppier than his healthier sister and had problems feeding, so the doctors wanted to keep a close eye on him. They told Cat and her husband Chito that although he was a good birthweight at 5 lb 10 oz, it had been crowded in the womb and Mari had been taking a lot of his nourishment from their mother.

Mari was released from hospital after a few days. Kai remained, but gradually put on weight and was released from hospital after a month, and it was expected that he would thrive at home. Except he didn't thrive at all. He was weak, he couldn't hold his head up like Mari did and barely moved when he was placed on the floor to play with his sister. Kai was still floppy and his hypersensitivity to sound and light left him screaming for hours, completely distraught.

Cat took her baby boy to the doctor many times. When Kai was six months old, she was told not to worry and that she was being an overprotective mother. When he was a year old, the doctor said that boys develop later than girls so it was only a matter of time before he caught up with Mari and met his developmental milestones. When he was two years old, he still hadn't even tried to speak. He was distant and didn't interact with anybody. Kai would spin a toy and sit and stare at it, or he would put his face close up to toys or people and look blankly into their eyes.

'I knew that there was something wrong with Kai, probably more than anybody because I had his sister of the same age to compare him with,' says Cat. 'She absolutely thrived. She was a chatterbox, she could crawl and walk early on, and she loved to play, yet Kai was the opposite. He didn't want to know anybody and he didn't like to play. I researched his symptoms all the time and I kept on coming back to autism because he was showing all the signs, yet his doctors couldn't agree on a diagnosis. It was incredibly frustrating and we didn't know what to do with him.'

When Kai reached three years of age, he became very sickly. He had pneumonia frequently, he developed lung cysts and he still wasn't interested in his surroundings or people, so he was evaluated by specialists once more. This time, he was deemed 'mentally disabled' and Cat was so angry with the label that she got a second opinion. Unfortunately, the second diagnosis was the same, yet Cat was still convinced that he was suffering from a severe form of autism as it seemed that he existed in a world of his own.

For a long time Kai didn't speak even one word. He would flap his arms around in frustration and headbang to communicate. It took two more years for the maternal diagnosis of severe autism to be confirmed and, while it was a relief, Kai had other problems to deal with. Around the same time, he was diagnosed with a large hole in his heart. After his heart surgery, he started to perk up and take an interest in what was going on around him. With more oxygenated blood running through his brain, Kai grew stronger, healthier and happier. However, it was once he had more energy that Cat had new issues and worries on her hands.

Kai ran away for the first time when he was five years old. Cat would turn around in a supermarket and he would be gone, wandering down the next aisle, without a care in the world. She would be in the park talking to a friend and the next minute, he would have disappeared into the woods on his own. Whenever he went missing, he would not respond to his name being called. He had no sense of danger and if he saw something in the distance that caught his eye, he would walk off without a second thought about leaving his mother or his sister.

One memorable day, they were in a park where there was a bouncy castle and he had an obsession with the inflatable attraction. Cat stopped to say hello to a friend and Kai took off again; he was gone in a matter of seconds. Cat was certain that he had gone to see the bouncy castle but, to her dismay, he wasn't there. She scoured the park, called his name and asked other parents if they had seen him. She had learned not to panic because he wandered off so frequently, but this time she was terrified that someone had taken him.

'I looked everywhere,' she remembers. 'I had other parents looking for him with me but – nothing. Usually, it didn't take long to find him but on this occasion, he wasn't in the obvious place, which was close to the castle. I was so frightened that he was gone that I got my phone out ready to call the police. I dialled 911 and I was just about to press the button, when I heard a parent say that a kid was on the bouncy castle with shoes on. It was my Kai. He hadn't thought to take his shoes off without me being there to tell him. The feeling of relief was immense and I couldn't even tell him off – all I could do was hug him.'

Kai disappeared many times. During his first year at school, he walked through the gates and off the school grounds. If it hadn't been for an eagle-eyed teacher who spotted him in the street, who knows where he might have ended up. On another occasion, Cat went to collect him from school and he wasn't in his classroom. His teacher radioed all the other teachers and asked them to look out for him, so he was eventually found safe and sound on the premises.

Short of tying him to her when they went out, there was little Cat could do except be extra vigilant at all times – even at home, as he was known to wander to neighbours' houses without telling her.

The turning point for Cat came when Kai was eight and they were on holiday in Seattle with her mother Kit and sister Donna. They were enjoying a day out at the zoo and Kai was walking up and down the steps, when Cat turned to fish something that she had accidentally dropped out of a litter bin. When she turned back around, he was gone.

Cat didn't worry at first. She walked to the bathrooms to see if he had walked over there because he was obsessed with them, but he was nowhere to be seen. They retraced their steps to see if he had gone back to any of the animal enclosures – still no sign of him. Cat enlisted the help of the zookeepers, who combed the area on their bikes, but it was like he had disappeared into thin air.

'My mum and sister were so upset,' says Cat. 'They were terrified that Kai might climb a fence or rails and get into an animal enclosure where he could have been attacked and killed. I tried to keep a steady head and I told myself that the zoo kept good enough security that no one could just get into the animal cages. I knew that there were lots of nooks and crannies that he could have climbed into, so I remained calm. After

 He couldn't understand why we were all so worried

thirty minutes of looking for him – the longest we've ever spent to find him – Mari was in hysterics, crying. In fact, we were all in a state, until a maintenance guy came over and told us that they had found him with the orangutan keeper.

When Kai saw us and we were all crying, he started laughing. He had no concept of what he had just done and he couldn't understand why we were all so worried. To him, he'd been on another of his little adventures and there was nothing the matter. I realised then that I couldn't go through with all the stress and worry of him running off. I had to do something to stop it before something really did happen to my son and he got hurt or worse.'

Cat read an article about service dogs and the difference they can make to an autistic child and their family. Unfortunately, she couldn't afford the massive adoption fees that ran into thousands of dollars, so she looked for other help. Eventually, she found a charity that agreed to work with her and Kai. Within two weeks, Cat received a phone call to say that they had a dog for them, a stray that had lived in and out of shelters for the duration of her young life. This animal was a female Wheaten Terrier, thought to be about 11 months old, who had been adopted by another family with an autistic child. After only eight months, she had been returned to the shelter because the family felt that she wasn't working out for them. The dog's sister had been adopted by a charity to train as a service dog, and the same charity then took in this dog to avoid her having to deal with the trauma of returning to the shelter.

It was obvious to the shelter staff that she had been neglected – possibly even abused – by her adopted family. She didn't do well on walks with other dogs and she found it hard to socialise in the dog park. She was particularly afraid of men, which was perhaps a hint that she had been beaten by one in the past.

As soon as Cat saw the young pup, she fell in love with her. She named her Kira. For the next few weeks, she worked with a dog trainer to make sure that the animal would be suitable for Kai. Kira took to the training straight away and it was obvious that she was highly intelligent and loved the interaction with Cat and her trainer. She was calm and friendly and she adored people.

'I couldn't believe that the other family had given her up,' says Cat. 'She was such a lovely dog, eager to learn and happy to be around. She was obedient so I knew that we wouldn't have problems with introducing her to Kai. She soon got over being timid around other dogs. She just needed a lot of love and attention to let her know that **Kai and Kira fell for each other the instant that she walked through the door** she was safe with us and that she could rely on us to feed and care for her. I couldn't wait to get her home.'

Kai and Kira fell for each other the instant that she walked through the door. At the time, Kai used the iPad to communicate and he told his mum he was happy to have her as his friend.

Kira would sit with him and follow him everywhere he went, which was good at first, but Kai soon tired of this and became anxious with the non-stop company. It was nothing that Kira had done, it was just Kai processing in his own way what was happening. He went through a phase of pushing her away from him when she would sit close. He would go in the bathroom and she would follow him then he would try to kick her away. Yet Kira would not leave him. She was incredibly stubborn and never stopped trying to get close to him and to win him over again. In the end, Kai stopped pushing her away and seemed to accept that Kira was a part of his life.

He started to feed her, which gave him a responsibility he had never known before and he liked the feeling of being a little bit in charge of something.

During their first walks, Cat would tie a leash around Kai's waist that was connected to Kira's so that she had full control over both her child and the dog and so that Kai also felt like he was walking the dog. He loved it. As the months went by, Cat stopped putting the leash around his waist and Kai started to walk the dog by holding the leash himself as his mum and sister walked with them, ready to step in if there was a problem.

Kai's habit of running off decreased significantly when Kira arrived on the scene. At first, if he tried it, Kira would pull back on the leash to tell Cat that he was starting to run. With the extra pair of eyes, it became easier for Cat to control his movements, particularly since he was attached to the other end of Kira's lead. Often Kai would think about running away but when he realised that Kira was pulling against him, he would stop and, gradually, he started to focus on the dog more than his desire to take off on one of his adventures.

Kira was somebody else for the young boy to consider – when he was distracted, he had to think twice because he was in charge of his dog who needed him. Slowly but surely, the pair formed a bond that is so strong they are virtually inseparable now.

Kira goes to school with Kai three days a week and has helped him to focus on his studies. She has proven herself to be a calming and steadying influence because she gives him the confidence to be away from home and everything else that is familiar.

She sleeps on his bed most nights. Cat sometimes sleeps on the floor next to Kai's bed because he suffers from asthma, so she likes to monitor him if he's been ill with a cold or has had trouble breathing during the day. Often, if Kai has breathing difficulties, Kira wakes up Cat to let her know. Once, Cat was sleeping in Mari's room for a girls' night sleepover when Kai had a full-blown asthma attack. Kira ran into Mari's room, barking loudly to alert Cat that her son was in trouble.

From the moment we got her,
it was like magic was happening

Kira anticipates Kai's moods and the need to protect him wherever they are, whether they're at school, in the street or at home.

'From the moment we got her, it was like magic was happening,' says Cat. 'She has all but cured him of taking off on his own and putting us all through hell. He rarely goes off on his own these days and if he does, she's close by. We're working on Kai becoming more independent and less dependent on me. I've always done everything for him but with Kira, I feel that he has a chance to one day be able to go out of the house on his own and walk to see a friend down the street without me or Mari. Kira gives me such a peace of mind when I'm not around Kai because I know that where he is, she is too, and she won't let him out of her sight. She intuitively knows her job and she takes it seriously. I can take her anywhere with us and I trust her with Kai's life. That little dog has worked miracles in our family. I'm so glad that we found her. She goes to show that shelter pets have a huge purpose in all our lives and can be the best pets of all. Our Kira is such a huge part of our family and we love her more than she will ever know.'

CHAPTER 21

- -

STEVE AND NANDI'S STORY

Steve was in the prime of his career as a speech specialist when he suffered his first leg tremor. He was also suffering from severe back pain and tiredness and he feared the worst. His mother had died from ALS (or amyotrophic lateral sclerosis, a form of motor neurone disease), a progressive neurodegenerative disease that affects nerve cells in the brain and the spinal cord. The condition can be hereditary, and Steve was terrified he had developed the same painful disease that killed her.

Steve, from California, booked himself in with a neurologist and, after numerous tests, he was told that he didn't have ALS but he was fast developing Parkinson's disease, a different progressive disorder of the nervous system. It affects movement, causing tremors, trembling in the hands, feet and legs, and impaired balance and coordination.

'When he said it wasn't ALS, I was elated,' recalls Steve. 'I watched my mother suffer and it wasn't pretty. It's a terrible disease and back then there was very little doctors could do to ease her symptoms. But then I researched Parkinson's disease and I realised that's not so good either. The good thing was that I was in the early stages and I was otherwise fit and healthy, so unlike ALS, it wasn't exactly a death sentence.'

Within a year, Steve was taking medication to ease his symptoms but he managed to keep working for another five years, until he retired in 2010 because he struggled to write reports due to hand tremors. Steve badly missed his work and struggled to cope with his developing illness. It was a slow progression but when walking became difficult because his balance was so compromised, he was devastated. Being unable to walk properly was something that Steve had been dreading more than anything because he knew that his life would change for the worst as he lost some of his independence. He found having to be pushed around in a wheelchair depressing and simple things like leaving the house required a marathon effort, so Steve started to stay in more, choosing not to socialise with friends.

It was no surprise that Steve changed. Without work, he was a little lost. Steve and his wife Kae had always been sociable people who enjoyed visiting friends and going out at weekends for date nights, but now just getting out of the house was fraught with difficulties. He tried his best to be optimistic but it was hard to remain upbeat when he couldn't walk properly and even simple tasks like getting dressed were near impossible sometimes.

Three years after Steve retired, Kae read an article about a lady in San Diego who suffered from Parkinson's; like Steve, she was pretty much housebound and very lonely. She had limited mobility but she acquired a dog from a small charity that adopted unwanted dogs and trained them to become helpers for people with all manner of disabilities. The organisation was called Shelter Dogs to Dream Dogs and was run by an animal behavioural expert called Cate Sacks. She had trained dogs to be aids to people with conditions ranging from autism to arthritis and cerebral palsy. The dog had helped the woman in the article so much

Her life had been turned around

that her life had been turned around. She was more confident, outgoing and had her social life back because she was able to leave her house. Kae had watched Steve's deterioration over the last few years and was inspired by the article to find something to give him back his spark for life.

'A dog could really help you, Steve,' said Kae. 'Why don't we give this woman a call and see what she has to say?'

With nothing to lose, the couple decided to pay Cate Sacks a visit. Together they discussed Steve's needs, agreeing that ideally he would have a larger dog to assist with his balance issues. Cate was eager to help and promised to find him a good match.

It didn't take her long to discover an unwanted two-year-old Rhodesian Ridgeback who she believed had the potential to be Steve's companion. The dog had been found running loose around San Diego and had been taken in by a local shelter. She was a gorgeous pure-bred dog, probably worth at least $1,000, yet no one had enquired after her at the shelter. The minute Cate saw her, she had a feeling that this big bundle of fur was destined to be the animal for Steve. For the next six weeks, Cate worked with the beautiful girl to get her ready for Steve and she was amazed at her intelligence and how quickly she learned her role. The dog picked up her commands very quickly, like it was second nature to her.

When she was ready to be introduced to her new owners, Steve and Kae travelled to San Diego and spent ten days with Cate so that they could learn together exactly what this animal could do for Steve.

'We did a lot of training going up and down stairs and in elevators,' recalls Steve. 'When I'm not in the wheelchair, I need help walking. I need a steady hand if I lose my balance. We went to so many bars and restaurants to see how quiet she was and she did her job wonderfully. Not once was she distracted by people or noises or the smell of food on people's plates. I knew I could take her anywhere and she wouldn't fail me. We called her Nandi after an African Zulu queen from the eighteen-hundreds. Her breed is African and Nandi was the mother of a great Zulu warrior, so we thought the name was fitting for her. I remember the first time we saw her, she was so big and she had bonded with Cate. I worried that she might not bond with me as she had taken to Cate so much, but after the ten days she knew what her purpose was.'

Except for suffering mild separation anxiety from Cate, Nandi soon settled into her new home.

For Steve, she was a welcome distraction from his regular routine. He didn't have time to sit in his chair and dwell on his Parkinson's disease, wondering which movement he would lose next.

Now he had a companion who relied on him for everything from walking to feeding and grooming, and this responsibility transformed his mindset. Steve had a purpose again and it made him feel good. When he got up at 5.30 a.m. because he couldn't sleep, Nandi would be there with him, bright as a lark, ready to start the new day. She loves to pick up clothes and towels for Steve and even his shoes when he can't quite bend down far enough to grab them.

It didn't take long for Nandi to change Steve's life for the better, just like the dog in the article.

He started to leave the house more regularly, with Nandi by his side. If he was in his wheelchair she would walk calmly next to him, ready to help him when he stood up. Sometimes his feet freeze up when he's walking and she stops immediately so that he can grab hold of her to steady himself then continue to walk. Nandi has established herself as Steve's safety crutch.

Together, the pair go anywhere and everywhere, so he is less isolated socially. If they visit a bar or restaurant, Nandi carefully navigates him through the crowds and safely around the tables.

They jointly fundraise for the Michael J. Fox Foundation, a charity set up by the actor, a famous Parkinson's sufferer, for research into the disease.

Everywhere they go, Nandi is a talking point. She's very striking to look at, tall with big eyes that shine brightly, and people feel compelled to stop and ask Steve what breed she is. Steve appreciates the attention being diverted from his wheelchair to his dog.

During Steve's brain surgery to insert electrodes to aid brain stimulation, a quiet and downcast Nandi sat in the waiting room with Kae and their daughters Malia and Alika, ready for Steve to come out. When he was wheeled into recovery after surgery, Nandi was there to lick his hand. As soon as she heard his voice, she perked up as if she knew he was going to be OK.

'Before I had Nandi, I didn't realise exactly what the power of a good dog can do,' says Steve. 'I thank God every day that Cate found her in the shelter because otherwise she might have been put down and our paths wouldn't have crossed. Nandi is a very loving dog and she takes her responsibilities very seriously. It amazes me how, despite her being such a big dog, she's gentle and careful when we're out. She can pick her way through a crowded room and I know I'll always be safe. Beyond her practical help, she saved me in more ways than I could ever have imagined. Parkinson's disease is a very personal illness and I get good days and bad days – she knows when I'm feeling low. Nandi rescued me just as much as she was rescued from the streets. I couldn't be without her now – she's such a big part of my family and my life. When it's just the two of us and she lets me pet her huge brown head, I couldn't be more content. Having Parkinson's disease doesn't have to be a death sentence – not when you have a dog like Nandi.'

> *she saved me in more ways*
> *than I could ever have imagined*

CHAPTER 22

- -

JANINE AND VYLKIS'S STORY

When 20-year-old Janine joined the US Army in 1983, she knew that this was a lifelong career choice because she wanted to make a difference. This well-educated young woman turned down a university scholarship to serve her country and enlist as a member of an elite combat training division, where she trained to become a combat telecommunications specialist, or a 'jumper'.

As a member of a Special Forces unit, she underwent extensive combat training in which she was taught to send and receive communications in a war zone or a hostile environment, and to destroy equipment if necessary to prevent it from getting into enemy hands. She was also trained to parachute into situations with Special Forces teams and Delta Force, and how to act as a sharpshooter. It was a demanding, dangerous job because Janine held the lives of her comrades in her hands in some of the world's most remote, hostile areas.

There were only five other women serving in the male-dominated Special Forces at the time, so the fact that Janine had been chosen for this role was a huge compliment and an incredible opportunity. The job presented major challenges for Janine. She suffered from vertigo but had to dismiss her fear of heights when she was asked to climb down the side of a 75-metre tower. Janine managed it, much to her relief, but she knew that there would be even more difficult challenges ahead. She also knew that, as a woman, plenty of colleagues were waiting for her to fail. She quickly learned that just because she had earned her green beret, it didn't mean that she automatically received respect from her peers or her bosses. Most of the men she served with were supportive, even if they didn't believe that a woman should be in their unit. The less supportive male minority caused problems for Janine in the ugly form of sexual harassment.

'I still remember it as clearly as if it were yesterday,' recalls Janine. 'It was hard enough doing the hugely demanding work, yet alone dealing with sexual innuendoes all the time and men who leered or made jokes about my body. I tried to stay focused but the reality was that it was difficult to handle without wanting to make a scene.'

A higher-ranking officer took Janine's harassment to the next level when he ensured that she worked closely with him whenever possible. As a naive 21-year-old, Janine didn't always see the hidden messages he was sending by singling her out to be his favourite. One afternoon, he managed to get Janine on her own in a small office space on the pretence that they had files to sort out. While they were alone, he beat and raped her. Tragically, she felt like she had to let it happen.

'I look back and sometimes I think that I should have fought back, but honestly, at the time, I was sure that if I had tried to escape, he would have killed me and covered up my death as some kind of an accident,' says Janine. 'I remember praying to God that it be over as quickly as possible and that he would leave me alone to pick myself up and get on with the job I was doing.

After he raped me, he whispered in my ear, "If you tell anyone what happened, I will find you and I will kill you. Do you understand?" I remember I nodded, desperately trying not to break down and cry my eyes out. I felt so violated and helpless. This man had completely abused his position to hurt me but there was nothing that I could do about it. Instead, as I left that room, I decided that I would pretend that the rape had never happened and if I could push it to the very back of my mind, I would be able to get on with my life. So I kept the secret for more than twenty years.'

On the completion of her training, a fragile Janine was sent to Fort Bragg, where she was assigned to the first unit that needed a combat airborne telecommunications specialist. In Signal Company, 5th Special Forces Group (Airborne), she was one of only five women in the battalion of 275 men.

The sexual harassment became more intense here and, after a different higher-ranking officer touched her breasts and bottom several times as she walked past, she filed a complaint. It fell apart immediately because it was impossible to prove, and she decided to live with it rather than jeopardise her career. As quickly as her complaint fell apart, so did Janine. She cried every morning because she didn't want to go to work. Janine tried to avoid her commander but that was extremely difficult, and she couldn't talk to anyone because the ranks closed against her. Ever the professional, she felt that she had to take it and get on with her job. It was a nightmare existence.

In February 1987, Janine left the army after a parachute jump went wrong. She was on a training exercise with other soldiers in her unit when she landed in a tree during a descent from a helicopter. Unable to release herself from the tree, she hung there for two hours until help arrived. When a soldier cut her loose, she fell onto the ground so hard and awkwardly that she injured her tail bone and compressed several vertebrae. This caused degenerative joint disease that eventually led to Janine needing a wheelchair due to the excruciating pain she suffers when she walks.

Janine left the army not only with severe physical injuries but also deep-seated mental torture. Although she married, the union failed because she struggled to be intimate with a man. She couldn't forget or put the rape and sexual molestation to the back of her mind when she was alone with a man.

'Sadly, all the memories came back when I became involved with any man,' says Janine. 'I couldn't be touched by anyone, so it really played a huge part in my divorce from my husband. The memory of the confident, empowered young woman I had been when I first entered the army had long gone and I was just a shell of the person I once was.'

As the years went by, Janine's back grew worse and so did her mental anguish. She began to suffer from horrific panic attacks that made her feel as though she was dying. She suffered severe post-traumatic stress disorder, of which nightmares were a key, persistent feature. These were so intense that she would wake up crying or sweating, her heart beating so hard it felt like it would leap out of her body.

She was frightened to go out, even with company, in case something happened to her when she left the safety of her apartment. Janine's home became a sanctuary that she avoided leaving even though she didn't like being indoors all the time; it became all she had. Her apartment has an enormous window that looks out onto the Chicago skyline and a beautiful green park. Janine would sit for hours looking at this amazing view, wishing that she could be a part of it. The therapist who was treating her for PTSD and severe depression constantly encouraged her to get out there into that park, where she could smell the trees and say hello to the people who walked through it.

'Sometimes I managed to get to the front door downstairs but that was as far as I would go,' recalls Janine. 'I'd sit for a little while, tears rolling down my face, and watch all sorts of passers-by go by my apartment complex. I wished more than anything that I could be brave like I used to be when I was in the army and wheel myself out of that building. I particularly loved to watch the people walking their dogs or those playing fetch with their beloved companions, the look of happiness clearly etched on their faces as they moved together, or enjoyed a big hug and a kiss. I longed to be them. I wished that I had a dog who would be there for me, my constant companion in the solitary world I had created for myself. But there was no way I ever would have a dog of my own. It wasn't practical, so I carried on in my own little apartment, sleeping a lot because I had no one to talk to.'

Janine lived an incredibly lonely life. In some ways, it wasn't a life at all but merely an existence in the bubble that she had created for herself. Once a week she saw her therapist and sometimes her sister Stacy would pop in for a chat. She got into the habit of having groceries delivered to her apartment so she didn't even have to venture out for food. She was taking so many tablets every day – one to beat the depression, another to control the PTSD, something else to help her to sleep, another for the pain in her back…

Then, in spring 2012, she was at her local veterans' hospital for her weekly therapy when a lady stopped her in the corridor and told her about an upcoming special event to promote sporting activities for wheelchair-bound veterans.

'I'm not interested, thank you,' said Janine.

'It's a great opportunity to meet other people,' the lady persisted. 'We can even arrange for a car to pick you up.'

The lady was so enthusiastic that Janine reluctantly agreed to go, a decision she regretted when she was back in the safety of her own home. The thought of meeting other people filled her with absolute terror and she wished she hadn't signed up.

Yet at the back of her mind, something was telling her that she had to go because she wouldn't regret it. Janine ended up attending the event and it was one of the best decisions of her life.

There were more than five hundred people in the conference room when she arrived and the noise was deafening. Janine could see swarms of people everywhere and she wanted to walk out as her heart started racing and she began to shake. She was starting to have a panic attack, so she backed her wheelchair up against the wall and sat there with her head in her hands, praying it would stop quickly.

As she sat there, she felt a cold, wet nose on her knee. When she opened her eyes, she saw a dog sitting right in front of her, his beautiful head resting peacefully on her lap. For a few seconds Janine was dumbstruck, then her fear disappeared and her heart rate started to slow down as she looked into two huge brown, friendly eyes. They stared at her as if to say, 'Don't worry, you're safe. I'm here.'

It turned out that the dog belonged to a veteran called Jay, who had witnessed the encounter.

'You need a service dog,' he said. 'My dog is specially trained to go everywhere with me. I left the army with severe PTSD and he's trained to help me to deal with it and to live a more normal life.'

Janine was shocked – how could a dog do all that? Was it possible that his dog really had saved him from a desperately dark time in his life?

Jay said that his dog had come from an organisation called War Dogs Making it Home, a charity set up by a lady called Elana Morgan, who rescued stray dogs and 'last chance' dogs on death row at their local shelters, and trained them to help veterans lead a better life.

Jay put Janine in touch with Elana and, although she was scared that she was doing the wrong thing, there was no denying that Jay's dog had made her feel much better during her panic attack.

Elana said that she had a dog called Vylkis, an enormous German Shepherd, rescued from a man in the Midwest – his owner had fallen on bad times and needed to find a home for his dog. When Vylkis arrived at Elana's home, he was terribly thin and in need of a lot of TLC. He quickly recovered and Elana thought he would be an ideal candidate to train for the War Dogs Making it Home programme.

Janine was invited to go to the training headquarters to meet Vylkis to see how they would get on. She fell in love with him instantly. He was a big dog but he was gentle and good on the lead, so Elana said she shouldn't have any problems taking him out while she was in a wheelchair.

They trained together for several weeks to be certain that they were a good match, which was confirmed. While they trained, Janine started to feel more positive about herself and her confidence was boosted. Getting out of bed in the morning wasn't such a chore – Janine wanted to get up because it meant she got to see Vylkis and she really looked forward to visiting him at the training centre.

Vylkis had a huge impact on Janine's life. Within two hours of arriving home, he helped her to fulfil a dream – they went to the park together. Vylkis is trained to walk beside her wheelchair and, as she wheeled herself onto the busy street below her apartment window, her nerves disappeared as he took charge. They crossed the road and took a half-hour walk around the park, just like anyone else.

'It was like being born again,' says Janine. 'I could smell the flowers in the pretty flower beds, I could touch the trees and I could look up into the blue sky and see the big, fluffy white clouds.

'The colours were magnified and I loved every second of that walk. People came up to me to say how beautiful my dog was and he did his job – he stood close by me and didn't let anyone get too near to me, like a four-legged guard just for me.'

The pair have come a long way since that first walk in the park. Vylkis has given Janine back everything that she lost during her depression. He is by her side every hour of

Vylkis has given Janine back everything that she lost during her depression

every day, no matter what. Janine suffers from sleep apnoea, so sometimes she stops breathing in bed. He lies next to her and he licks her face if she stops breathing so that she wakes up immediately. Nowadays Janine rarely suffers from panic attacks or severe anxiety because of her constant companion. If she gets stressed, Vylkis rests his big head on her lap so that she can cuddle him – the feel of his fur and the look in his eyes calms her immediately, and his touch is far more effective than any anxiety pill.

With Vylkis by her side, Janine goes out whenever she feels like it and doesn't mind being around strangers or other people any more. Distracting attention away from Janine, Vylkis is the icebreaker that starts many happy conversations – about where he came from, what a beautiful dog he is – and Janine adores *this* attention.

'We have such a bond together,' says Janine. 'I have to get up and take him for a walk. I can't lie in bed for hours or sit in my chair watching the world go by. Vylkis needs to be fed and watered; he needs to get out of the apartment just as much as me. It's funny really, because Elana saved him when he needed it the most and she gave him a purpose in his life – me! In turn, he has given me my purpose in life so you could say that we saved each other. I am so lucky to have found my Vylkis and I love him more than life itself. He's the best thing that has ever happened to me because he saved me from myself.'

CHAPTER 23

LYNETTE AND CONNOR'S STORY

High school sweethearts and newlyweds Lynette and Shawn put their dreams of having their own family on hold while they enjoyed a few years with just the two of them. They always planned to have two children, maybe more, when the time was right. In the meantime, they settled on having a dog to keep Lynette company when Shawn worked away from home.

Lynette's family loved cats but she personally had dreamed of having a dog, and that dream came true when the couple bought their first dog, Bella, a chocolate Labrador, from a breeder in Virginia. Their joy was short-lived as Bella died of kidney failure at just two years old. Losing Bella broke Lynette's heart and it took her nine months before she could even contemplate having another dog in the house. When her mind was made up that she was ready for another dog, she decided that she wanted to rescue a needy dog from a shelter rather than buy another from a breeder. Shawn was all for adopting the right pup to fill the quiet in their house that Bella had left behind.

They had never been to a high-kill shelter before and both were nervous about what they were going to find. Lynette knew she was going to want to take every single one of those abandoned dogs, so she steeled herself for the difficult task ahead of picking out just one pup.

'I have a big heart and I'm easily upset, particularly where animals are concerned,' says Lynette. 'I tried to prepare myself by picking out a few possible dogs from the shelter's website so I wouldn't feel so overwhelmed when we got there. As I'd imagined, it was hard walking past so many poor dogs in need of a home. I wished I could have taken them all – it was depressing seeing so many unwanted dogs all in one place. A high-kill dog shelter is one of the most soul-destroying places you can ever see because when you've visited, you start to lose a little of your faith in human kindness.'

One puppy stood out for Lynette: a tiny, jet-black pup, who was skin and bones he was so thin. He was very quiet and subdued, which gnawed at Lynette's heartstrings – weren't puppies supposed to be full of life and energy? This poor boy grabbed her arm when she held him, refusing to let go when she tried to put him back in his cage. The shelter staff informed them that he was a Labrador–Great Dane mix but seeing him lying there, desperate for love and attention, it was hard to imagine that he might grow into a huge dog one day. For now, he looked pathetic.

'Let's take him,' Lynette said to Shawn. 'He needs us!'

Shawn didn't take much persuading and they signed up for him on the spot. It was several weeks before he went home with them, though, because he fell ill with a virulent strain of pneumonia – in fact, they almost lost him. Lynette visited him at the shelter every day until he was allowed home. It was then that she and the puppy she named Connor really connected. She showed him what it was like to have a nice meal, toys and a cosy bed, and he lapped up all the love she showered him with.

Soon after Connor arrived home, Shawn was sent to the Bahamas for work for several months at a time. Those were tough days without him – Lynette missed her husband dreadfully and nights at the house were lonely without human company. Sometimes they would speak on the phone to say hello but for the most part, they didn't have a lot of contact. Shawn worked long hours to make strict deadlines as a chartered surveyor in the Bahamas, where the telephone service was horrendous and as he didn't live near a town he had no Internet connection.

Connor became Lynette's best friend and she was so thankful to have him to occupy her time and to keep her from feeling too lonely in the house. He would snuggle up to her on the sofa and put his soft head on her lap as they watched TV together. He would follow her everywhere, as if he were keeping an eye on her, and having him there gave her a greater sense of security. Lynette felt sure that if anyone were to try to break into the house, they would have Connor to deal with.

Connor was such an obedient, quiet dog that Lynette was allowed to take him to the gym where she worked at the reception. There were many times when clients would not even know he was there because he was so well behaved, and those who did know him loved his laid-back and gentle manner when they petted him. By this time he had grown into a huge animal yet he was such a gentle giant, as if he knew that if he didn't behave he wouldn't be allowed to accompany Lynette to work. He was like her own personal bodyguard who took his job very seriously.

'I truly believe that this was his way of saying "thank you for rescuing me",' says Lynette. 'While Shawn wasn't around, Connor took on the role of my guardian, my protector. He was such an old soul. I never formally trained him to do anything. I would just talk to him and ask him to come with me. I don't think I ever raised my voice and he was as sharp as any human. Connor was the best company I kept, that's for sure!'

Lynette suffered from bouts of severe anxiety for which she took medication. These periods were worsened by Shawn's absence but as soon as Connor came into her life, she found that she was able to manage her symptoms more effectively. If she was feeling overwhelmed at work, or if she needed a good cry at home after a particularly stressful or draining day, Connor was there to lick her tears away; on days like those, he would never leave her side.

As Shawn was away so much, Connor accompanied Lynette wherever she went and whatever she was doing. He enjoyed holiday dinners with the rest of the family, and it was Connor who cured Lynette's grandmother's profound fear of big dogs, which stemmed back to her girlhood.

The day finally came when Lynette and Shawn felt that the time was right to try for a baby, having decided that since they were both in their thirties and Lynette's proverbial biological clock was ticking, they couldn't wait much longer. However, what the couple thought would come naturally and quickly turned into frustrating years of doctors' appointments, surgeries, fertility treatments and hormones when Lynette couldn't get pregnant.

'I felt unhappy the whole time because I felt like I was failing to produce our much-wanted child,' says Lynette. 'Having a baby became an obsession, particularly for me. I had a calendar where I had all the dates when it would be a good day to try for a baby, which isn't the least bit romantic! As a result, my moods were all over the place. I was happy one minute and crying my heart out the next. I would look at mums with their kids in the street and feel a deep sadness that it wasn't me. I began to question why life was so unfair. We were ready for a family and we knew we would give a child everything it would need in the world, yet God wasn't

Deep down I was hurting so badly, it was almost tearing me apart

granting our deepest wishes. I tried to be happy for friends who became pregnant, I really did, but deep down I was hurting so badly, it was almost tearing me apart.'

To make matters worse, although Shawn was now back home, he was working night shifts, leaving Lynette home alone with too much time to think. As a lifelong sufferer of depression and anxiety, this was not a good place for her to be in. She would become desperately sad and angry; on bad nights she sometimes had to fight the urge to punch a wall with frustration. Sleep didn't come easily as thoughts raced through her head until the early hours of the morning.

The one thing that kept Lynette going – and calm – was Connor. Even on the really bad days, he was Lynette's big furry shoulder to cry on. He was always there for Lynette, happy to sit on her lap on the sofa – even though he weighed in at 40 kg. It was the way he would look at her with his deep brown eyes, as if he truly understood what emotional turmoil she was going through. Connor instinctively tuned in to Lynette's mood swings and unhappiness, just like a human.

After years of trying for a baby, the couple were told that Lynette needed a hysterectomy to cure the painful endometriosis she was suffering from. Being told that she needed such a huge operation, one that would effectively end any chances of having a child, was a huge blow and Lynette fell into a depression. She couldn't accept that there was no pill to miraculously make her pregnant, no surgery that could help. The finality of her situation was devastating because she had never imagined her life without a child.

Around the same time, Shawn lost his job – and with it the couple's health insurance, so a hysterectomy was unrealistic given the huge costs involved. The couple reluctantly decided that it was in their best interests to give up their fight to have a child. They had been told by every doctor they had seen that it just wasn't going to happen for them. The emotional turmoil was putting an enormous strain on their once close relationship so it was time to focus on something else, otherwise they felt that they would end up divorced within a year.

In a way it was almost a relief: no more surgeries, no more hospital visits, no more hormone drugs that were playing havoc with Lynette's moods. She decided to let her body recover and get fit, so she started working out more, which increased her sense of well-being.

For their fresh start, they moved into a small house on five acres of land, where they kept a horse and enjoyed the pleasures of rural living. Without the pressure of trying for a baby, Lynette focused on other things, such as her job, her horse and her relationship with Shawn, which had suffered so much in the past few years.

Their quality of life improved – until Lynette got sick. She had a stomach bug which kept her at home for days because she felt so ill, throwing up every morning and feeling wretched. Shawn suggested she might be pregnant but she laughed off this suggestion; when the doctors told her that getting pregnant was impossible, she believed them.

Against all the odds, Lynette found out that she was pregnant, something she had thought impossible even in her wildest dreams. It can sometimes happen that women who have struggled to fall pregnant do then fall pregnant naturally once they take the pressure off themselves, and this seemed to be the case with Lynette.

Connor seemed to know that things were very different with Lynette from the moment she started getting sick.

'He would follow me around the farm or the house, always staying close by me, like he was protecting me and our unborn child,' recalls Lynette. 'I remember someone telling me I would have to consider getting rid of him once the baby came because I couldn't possibly have a huge dog around a small child. I also remember giggling to myself. While I had many fears of becoming a new parent, Connor being around our child was never one of them. If anything, I worried he would feel left out or neglected since he had been with me through so much. I always knew that he would be amazing with our baby. There was never a doubt in my mind.'

Lynette gave birth to a beautiful baby girl, Callan, who is truly the apple of Connor's eye. Just like a big brother, he is protective of her too. From the moment she arrived home from the hospital, Connor rarely left her cot. They go for walks every day and he stays proudly by her side, acting as her guardian and protector.

And Callan loves her big brother. As a baby she used him to get on her feet to take her first steps; now she lavishes him with affection whenever he is close, which is virtually the whole time. Often, these days, Lynette finds him snoozing on the couch, covered in toys that have been gifted to him by her daughter.

Although Connor is ageing and becoming arthritic and slower now, he will still happily play with his toys and bark at his human family at night for some playtime or a nice marrow bone – he is still young at heart.

'He has been a part of so much of my life and I owe so much happiness to him,' says Lynette.

'Even as he snores next to me, he makes me feel at peace. I hope everyone can have a companion even half as amazing as he is and I pray he knows how much he's loved. Even I couldn't have imagined the bond we would develop that day I picked him out of the shelter. It is hard to imagine my life without him and I secretly wish for a magic spell to keep him with me forever.'

— **"** —

Even I couldn't have imagined the bond we would develop that day I picked him out of the shelter

CHAPTER 24

JIM AND JESS'S STORY

When Val met her future husband Jim, he had his own kennel of dogs in his garden. Brought up in a house that always had dogs, it was no surprise Jim loved his animals. In the 1950s he bred Wire Hair Fox Terriers to show at Crufts, the biggest dog show in the world, which at that time held its annual show in Blackpool, England. He was quite successful with this, until his decision to stop the breeding on discovering that fellow competitors were employing cruel methods for their dogs to win, such as making them walk on needles to improve their posture, and feeling that the industry wasn't doing enough to stop it. Jim felt so disheartened that he just kept his dogs as pets, then, when he married Val and they had children, he always rescued his dogs from shelters in order to give the 'underdogs' a home with them, in Poynton, Cheshire.

'He always said he felt better giving an unwanted dog a home, rather than buying from a breeder,' recalls Val. 'From being in the breeding industry, Jim had come across some scoundrels who were only in it for the money and I think he wanted to be as far away from that world as he could. So we adopted our pets from the local animal homes or from people who didn't want them any more – the types who would have dumped them without another thought for their chances of survival.'

The last dog Val and Jim had owned together was a black collie mix called Jess. Their previous much-loved dog, Tess, had died of old age. Jim was heartbroken – so much so that he told Val and their grown-up kids, Sharon and Steven, that under no circumstances was he going to get another dog.

'It's too painful when they go,' he said. 'I just can't do it any more.'

Jim was a man who kept his feelings close to his chest but Val had seen him cry many a time over a dog, so this time she knew how hard he must be hurting when he said goodbye to Tess. However, as many people will testify after losing a family pet, their house felt empty and lifeless after Tess passed away. Jim was miserable and it was far too quiet for anyone's liking. He missed having a constant canine friend around to walk and to talk to in the daytime when Val worked and he was on his own. Grieving the loss of his friend, Jim became withdrawn, lost in his own thoughts and the memories of the dog who stole his heart.

He didn't go out for his twice-daily walks and became incredibly lonely because, for the first time in his life, he was without a dog. The truth was, he would have loved any dog that turned up at their house – he just needed a little persuasion that a dog was the best thing for him, the perfect remedy to help him come to terms with losing Tess.

Steve and Sharon decided that, despite what Jim said, he was going to have another dog – and they would get it for him. Sharon saw puppies advertised in her local newspaper, the *Worcester Evening News*, and she and her husband Dave went to see if any of the dogs would be suitable for Jim. Sharon was supposed to check out the puppies and report back to Val but the reality didn't quite work out like that.

The farmer who had the puppies took them out to a stable in his barn to see the little bitch, but she was too timid to come out and huddled herself into the hay in the dark corner. When the farmer dragged her out roughly, Sharon spotted huge red welts under her belly where it looked like she had been whipped with a riding crop. The farmer said that if they didn't take her right there and then, she would be killed with a spade or sent to a shelter because he didn't want an extra mouth to feed.

'Besides,' he said, 'she's bloody stupid and I need a collie to work with my sheep. This one will never make the grade – I need to get rid of her.'

And that was it. Ever her father's daughter, Sharon paid the £50 adoption fee and drove her home, vowing to keep her if Jim didn't want her.

Jim was adamant that he didn't want the dog.

'I told you I couldn't have another one!' he said. 'I can't take the upset when they die. You'll have to keep it!'

After decades of marriage, Val knew that Jim didn't mean a word of what he said. She knew that he would come around as soon as he saw her – and how right she was!

The next weekend when Val and Jim went to visit Sharon, Jim stroked the puppy, who was shaking a little, probably afraid of men after the farmer had beaten her. Right up until the end of the weekend, Jim said he wasn't going to take her but then, as they said goodbye in the driveway, he looked at Sharon and said with a sheepish smile, 'Can I take Jess now?'

Jim and sweet Jess became inseparable very quickly. Where one was, the other was never far away.

It took him hardly any time to train her – she was such an intelligent little dog. Jim spoke to Jess like she was a human. He never commanded her to do anything; whatever the request, he asked her nicely and she always did as he asked, as if the pup the farmer had said was stupid understood everything.

With a new puppy to take care of, Jim, who had recently undergone open-heart bypass surgery, started to go out of the house more, which did wonders for his mindset. Twice a day they went for walks over the fields at the back of their house in Cheshire. He made friends with a group of people who walked their dogs over the fields at the same time he did. They would meet every morning and evening, and the dogs would play together while their owners chatted.

'It did Jim so much good to have Jess,' says Val. 'She gave him a spring in his step, a new meaning in his life, something to get up in the morning for – particularly when, after the surgery, he had struggled to get up sometimes because of the fatigue he felt. Our family might have saved Jess from a certain death at the hands of that awful farmer but she sure did give a lot more back to us than we could ever have given her. Getting out of the house and exercising gave Jim a renewed sense of energy and well-being. For the first time in a few years, he felt healthier than he had in a long time, and more cheerful too. If he went to bed early, then so did Jess. She slept at his feet every single night and even came on the bed sometimes when they were in the bedroom alone together. I honestly felt like this dog was sent to Jim for a purpose, like he was meant to have her. They had such a special bond and she made his life in his sixties fun with her endless energy and love for him and the whole family.'

Jim felt so fit and well that when he was diagnosed with stage four throat cancer in autumn 2004, it came as a huge shock. Nobody, not even Jim, had known he was sick until one day he had a pain in his chest every time he swallowed. By the time the cancer was discovered, it had already spread to his liver and lungs, and he was given a year to 18 months at best to live.

It was a tremendously difficult time for Val, as Jim went downhill rapidly as the disease took hold over his entire body. His family all fought to keep his spirits up and although the company of his granddaughters Emily and Molly helped, ultimately it was Jess who made all the difference in his last days on earth.

Jess followed him everywhere, even to the toilet. She would sit beside his feet as he sat in his chair in the corner of the room and he would rub her soft, sweet head for hours on end. If Jim was frightened, he never said a word; when he was with Jess, he was calm, often reflecting on his life and how he wouldn't have changed a thing. Jess would only move if he did, as if she were his guardian angel and it was up to her to keep him company at all times.

 I don't know what he was saying to her, but whatever it was, she understood and she was a comfort to him

There were days when Jim felt too sick to get out of bed but he forced himself to get up and walk Jess, even if it was only a few yards down the nature trail beside the family home. He would walk slowly because he was in pain, and she would walk beside him at the same speed – there was never a need for a leash.

'Sometimes I caught him talking softly to Jess with tears in his eyes and she would listen intently before she gently put her head in his hand or in his lap,' recalls Val. 'I don't know what he was saying to her, but whatever it was, she understood and she was a comfort to him. I wondered for a long time whether he talked to her about death. He often said to me that he wasn't afraid but that was all. I imagined him having the talk about the "other side" with his best friend.'

Jim walked Jess right up until a week before he died, three months after his diagnosis. He became desperately weak and was unable to get up even if he wanted to; the cancer had taken away every ounce of strength in his body. One of his friends from the dog walkers group came to walk Jess that week, but she always seemed reluctant to leave Jim.

'You go, Jess,' he would say with a wave of his hand. 'I'll still be here when you get back.'

'The day he died, she had been with him all night and all morning, only going out to relieve herself for a few minutes,' says Val. 'I think we all knew that the time was coming and she wanted to be with him. He was in and out of consciousness but he would reach his hand out to Jess, who would put her head into his hand and let him feel her, as if she were reassuring him that he wasn't alone and she was there for him to the end. Even after Jim passed away, she wouldn't leave the bedroom. I swear that she cried, although some people would laugh at me for saying that. I knew that she loved me but Jim was *her* human and she grieved just like we all did. It was just so sad seeing her sit in the bedroom, often on the bed where he had taken his last breaths.'

Jim's death was the hardest thing that Val had ever had to cope with. Gradually, Val and Jess started to come to terms with losing Jim, as they saw their way through the tears, the loneliness and the terrible void together. Just as she had been a best friend and a comfort to Jim, Jess was now Val's comfort. It was Jess who would keep Val company all the time, watching TV or reading a book in bed, or sitting in the living room with the memories of her beloved husband.

'She would sit next to me wherever I was,' Val says. 'I know that if I didn't have to walk her, I would have stayed in the house a lot more than would have been healthy for me after I lost Jim. Jess was my new constant and my reminder of a wonderful man. When she eventually died too, I was heartbroken again but I kept my promise to Jim on his deathbed. "Promise me that you'll put Jess's ashes with mine, Val," Jim had said. "She needs to be with me when she goes."'

Val kept her word. Putting Jess's ashes in a little box, she and Steve took her to West Bromwich in the Midlands, where Jim's ashes were buried with his grandma and grandad who had brought him up as a child. She dug a little hole in that grave and gently put sweet Jess's ashes into it. Val kept some ashes at home to scatter around the fields where she and Jim had spent most of their time together.

'I truly believe that Jess knew that she had been saved from a terrible fate and she repaid us by being the best dog anyone could wish for,' says Val. 'She was one in a million. Her loyalty was deep and true, and she gave us so much back. I still miss her to this day but it gives me enormous comfort thinking of her walking the fields in heaven with her best friend and mine, my dear Jim.'

CHAPTER 25

JESS AND BEAMER'S STORY

Moving house as a teenager involves upheaval, especially when their new home is many miles away from the place where they grew up. When Jess was 15, her mum, Vivian, told her that they were going to stay at their rental home in Orlando, Florida, for the summer – a thousand miles from Chicago, where Jess had lived all her life. What Vivian decided not to tell her straight away was that this was in reality a more permanent move.

Jess had been badly bullied and beaten up by a gang of girls from school, who attacked her mercilessly at the shopping mall. Vivian and her husband Spyro were running out of ideas about how to help their daughter, but they reasoned that she had always been happy on holiday in Florida, so a fresh start there seemed like a good plan.

The move took some getting used to for Jess.

'I was furious with my mother for dragging me away from my dad, my brother and everything I knew,' recalls Jess. 'She told me that we were staying in Florida at the end of the summer and it was a huge shock. I went crazy at her. I had always thought that we were just there for a long holiday. After I was beaten up and the police got involved, I had wanted to get as far away from Chicago as I could, but now I was healed, happy and ready to get back to some kind of normality. Looking back with the benefit of hindsight, it was a very brave decision for Mum to make because she left her family and friends too, but she did it to give me a new life where the bullies couldn't reach me. I can appreciate that now but at the time I missed Chicago so much.'

Living in Florida was hard for Jess. She missed her immediate family and close friends, and longed to get back to her vibrant home city. Starting a new school was difficult, especially because Jess tried to make friends but this takes time and she wasn't the patient type. Even the hot climate was a challenge after growing up in a much more variable one. It was Vivian who bore the brunt of Jess's temper tantrums as she blamed her mother for packing their bags and leaving behind the only world she knew.

A saving grace came in the shape of Jess's two horses, Cash and Clifford. She rode every day and spent endless hours at the barn with her two boys. Being around them kept her calm and focused. She made horsey friends in Orlando, which helped to make life more bearable.

One day just before her seventeenth birthday, Jess went to the barn with her dad, who was visiting from Chicago, to ride her horses. As they arrived, they noticed a huddle of people by the side of the road looking at something in the street. A female dog and two puppies, one boy and one girl, were causing the commotion. The mum looked like a spaniel and, judging by the sorry state of them, it appeared that they

I knew that he needed me as much as I needed him

had been strays for some time. Their coats were matted and filthy, and they stunk to high heaven. One of the puppies was slow and lethargic, as if starving or dehydrated. Jess picked up the little black and white male, a mixture of a spaniel and collie, and one look into his sad eyes was enough to convince her that she had to adopt him.

'I knew that this was the dog for me,' recalls Jess. 'He was so small and in need of love. Whereas his sister was vibrant and full of energy, he was quiet and sad-looking, like he had all the cares of the world on his shoulders. He melted my heart. I asked my dad if it was OK for me to keep him and he thought it was a great idea. I've always been a huge animal lover and Dad realised that a pup would go a long way to helping me come to terms with moving to Florida.

I took that little bundle of fur back home with me that day. We bathed him and I loved him. Honestly, looking into his sweet eyes was like staring into a kind-hearted soul and I knew that he needed me as much as I needed him.'

Jess named the pup Beamer and took him to the vet for a check-up as he was so quiet and withdrawn. He was estimated to be no older than four weeks, which in normal circumstances is far too young to be weaned off his mother's milk. His stomach and intestines were infested with worms and parasites, and he was suffering from a whole array of different infections, probably caused by a weakened immune system.

'If you hadn't taken him in, he would have been dead within a couple of days,' the vet told Jess. 'He was at death's door when you found him. He's very lucky to be alive.'

Beamer was fortunate to make a full and speedy recovery and, as if he was thankful to Jess for saving him, he never left her side. They became best friends in every sense of the word – and, for the first time since the move to Florida, she was completely happy.

Three months after she adopted Beamer, Jess fell hard while riding her young horse Cash. The accident snapped her leg clean in half and she was in a wheelchair for four months while her leg repaired from surgery. The rehabilitation period meant no more riding and no cheerleading practice at school. During this difficult time, she was picked on so badly by a group of girls that Vivian enrolled her in another school to finish her senior year. Jess's situation was miserable and painful. She couldn't drive her car to meet her friends; getting about in her cumbersome wheelchair was difficult; even the boy she was dating didn't stop by to see her, which made her more angry than sad.

The one who really stuck by Jess while she was healing was Beamer. He adored her. It didn't matter to him that she couldn't take him for long walks any more, that she couldn't pick him up easily to give him a cuddle. He didn't care that life was put on hold while she recovered because as long as they were together, he was in his happy place.

'Beamer saved me through that dark time,' says Jess. 'He didn't abandon me when I needed him. If anything, he was more attentive towards me, always looking up to check that I was OK. We would sleep together in bed and I would cry on his beautiful head. He wouldn't move or leave me unless I told him to. Just having him there for a hug when I felt sad and lonely was enough to cheer me up and to realise that I was lucky to have him.'

Four years after she adopted Beamer, sadness struck Jess again. Jess was a talented rider in the prestigious hunter show rings in Florida. She hoped that her beloved show horse Leo, a striking black gelding who had once belonged to the singer Janet Jackson, was going to take her to the top of the amateur rider circuit. Leo and Jess were an impressive team, winning nearly every competition they entered. They were working towards competing at national showjumping level when, without warning, Leo died from an illness.

After Beamer, Jess was closest to Leo so it was a huge shock when he died. She was left feeling empty, confused and angry. It seemed like only five minutes ago they were the team to beat and they were heading for national stardom! His death had shattered her dreams and she was left with the memories of a wonderful horse who she loved with every piece of her heart. It was like a light had gone out in her soul and she couldn't handle the loss.

In an attempt to escape the haunting grief, Jess turned to painkillers and sedatives. While they helped to mask her true feelings, once the effects had worn off she felt far worse. Jess also turned to alcohol, going out partying every night with her friends. Excessive drinking provided temporary relief from her sadness but the morning after a heavy session she felt wretched. For months she was like a zombie. Nothing really mattered any more; she wanted nothing and no one – apart from Beamer.

'My little black dog could take me to a place no one else could,' says Jess. 'He made me remember that living was OK, even when I felt like totally giving up, and there were many times I just wanted to curl into a little ball and die. I just couldn't see a point in carrying on. Beamer showed me that

He made me remember
that living was OK, even when
I felt like totally giving up

I was still loved and I still had a reason to love. How could I want to leave everything behind when that would have meant losing him too? His gentle reminders in the form of a cuddle, a lick and kisses saved me once again through the darkest of times. He pulled me through again.'

Beamer has been Jess's shoulder to cry on throughout hard times and heartbreaks. He helped her to transition from an angry, confused teenager into a caring, responsible adult and now mother to her son, Ryland. Beamer is still there for her when she sits down to take a breather at night, or to follow Ryland when he runs around their barn laughing joyously.

'He's the most exceptional dog I've ever encountered,' says Jess. 'I've never met a more pure and honest soul. Calling him my best friend for this long has been the biggest blessing. I feel so lucky that he chose me. We've been through some of life's biggest challenges together but the only thing that ever gives my soul any peace is knowing that, no matter what, he'll be with me until his dying breath. He's my Beamer, my best friend in the world, and he won't leave me to walk through this world alone. In years to come when he has to switch out for a younger body, I know he'll find me. And I know I'll know it's him by taking one look into those eyes; the eyes of the sweetest soul I'll ever know.'

CHAPTER 26

COURTNEY AND DIABLO'S STORY

When Courtney was a teenager, she often stayed for long weekends and summers at her cousin Lori's ranch in California. It was a beautiful place to visit and Courtney was close to Lori and her husband Doug. They had three horses and they enjoyed endless hours riding the trails near their home.

The only thing missing from the ranch was a dog, so when Lori heard about a beautiful black German Shepherd dog, the runt of the litter, who needed a home, she jumped at the chance to adopt him. Even though he was perfect in every way, his breeder decided that he wasn't show quality so she couldn't sell him. This meant that she had no use for the puppy and, as a result, she planned to take him to the animal shelter. A friend of hers stepped in and agreed to foster him, but the poor animal was subsequently passed around from one foster home to another. The 18-month-old pup's future was uncertain, until Lori and Doug heard about him and agreed to take in the homeless hound.

Diablo, as they named him, was emaciated when he arrived at their ranch. His previous neglect was all too clear: he was more than 20 kg underweight, literally skin and bone, with protruding bones and very little muscle, his fur was filthy and he had fleas all over his body. Yet as soon as he got out of the car and saw Lori and his new family, his eyes sparkled with excitement as if he knew that

He was home at last

this was it – he was home at last. His search to find humans to love him was over.

He settled in easily right from the start. He loved to follow Lori and Doug around the barn and he would watch when they rode the horses in the arena. Often he would go with them on trail rides, always walking a few steps behind, bringing up the rear as if he were protecting them and watching out for predators.

The ranch owners took him everywhere because, with such a laid-back personality, Diablo was a joy to have around. From camping trips in the mountains to shopping trips to the local town, he was often the centre of attention because this once half-starved pup grew into a huge dog, more like a big bear.

Diablo took a great shine to Courtney. Although he was a quiet dog, he would bark like crazy when she visited and he wouldn't let her out of his sight for the entire duration of her stay.

'I loved that dog as my own,' recalls Courtney. 'I always felt so close to him. When me and my brother Zack would visit, it was like he took on the responsibility of making sure we stayed safe.

Diablo never let me go out to see the horses on my own, and whenever I sat quietly watching TV or reading in the lounge, he would sit next to me with his head on my lap. I liked the feel of him being there close to me all the time. It felt safe.'

One wonderfully hot, balmy summer, when Courtney was 14 years old, the whole family went on a camping trip to Lake Shasta in Northern California. Courtney, Zack, their parents, Lori, Doug, plus Lori's parents, Jay and Marilyn, all went along for the ride. It was a week-long trip and they planned to enjoy the great outdoors in tents and a motorhome. Of course, Diablo went too and he loved the freedom of sleeping outside.

The two families hired a pontoon boat and spent most days on the crystal-clear water, basking in the heat of the blazing sun. One day, they moored the boat on the shore of the lake and Doug and Courtney jumped off to take Diablo for a walk. They wandered up the bank and into the woods so that they could all stretch their legs after being cooped up for hours on the boat. Diablo enjoyed exploring the thick vegetation and chasing birds.

Doug walked out in front while Diablo raced around, basking in the scenery. He was so obedient that he didn't need to be on a leash in the countryside, particularly as they were in the middle of nowhere. Courtney and Doug followed the trail and walked into an area thick with undergrowth. They had deviated slightly from the track and, as they walked, they suddenly became surrounded by thousands of bees. They realised they had inadvertently disturbed a huge bees nest as the irritated insects started stinging the three of them all over their bodies.

Doug had the foresight and presence of mind to run towards the lake, where he jumped into the water to get rid of the bees.

Courtney was less fortunate and chose to run back the way they had just walked. She was incredibly disorientated as she tried to fight off the bees that swarmed in her hair, under her swimsuit and in her shorts. As the bees repeatedly stung her, it felt as though she was being spiked by thousands of red-hot needles; unsurprisingly, she panicked. In all the confusion and drama, she couldn't think clearly and didn't know where she was as she ran deeper into the forest.

As she unsuccessfully batted the bees away from her face, she became aware that Diablo hadn't followed Doug to safety. Instead, he had stayed by her side and he was trying to protect her by chasing off the bees.

'I looked down and there was Diablo, right behind me,' Courtney remembers. 'He was trying to snap at the bees that were on my legs and back, like he thought he might stop them from hurting me. All the time the bees swarmed all over him, yet he refused to run away and leave me. I was screaming at the top of my voice because I was so frightened and he stuck

All the time the bees swarmed all over him, yet he refused to run away and leave me

around in all the chaos. At one point, he pushed his head into my hand and I think instinct made me grab his collar to steady myself. By this time I didn't know where I was but I could hear my parents calling for us, although I couldn't see them.'

Courtney and Diablo had been heading further into the woods away from the lake, but when Courtney grabbed hold of his collar, the dog took charge. Even though the bees were stinging them both everywhere, he didn't panic. He calmly led Courtney away from the woods and down to the lake, where their family was waiting to help.

Once they reached the lake, they both jumped into the water and the bees took their leave. Courtney's arms and torso were absolutely covered in bee stings. Underneath her hair, her scalp was bright red and bleeding in places. Diablo was in pain from the stings, too. The bees had attacked him mostly on his torso and also his head, which was swollen from the trauma.

In the shelter of the motorhome, they spent the evening covered in lotion and ice packs, snuggling and nursing their wounds together. Courtney couldn't stop thinking about the lucky escape she had just had.

'Diablo saved me,' says Courtney. 'He could have run off and followed Doug when the bees started to sting us but instead he chose to stay with me even though he was in severe pain himself. I could have got lost in those woods because I just ran to get away from those bees. I didn't know which direction I was really going in; I was just running blindly to escape. I could have fallen and broken a leg in the panic. Thankfully, Diablo kept calm and led me to safety. I still wonder what would have happened if he hadn't been there with me. I have no doubt that things could have ended up a lot worse. Whenever I see Lori and Doug, we still talk about what happened and they still reckon he was the best dog that they ever had. We always say that Diablo was a dog who went above and beyond for the people he loved, as if he was grateful for being rescued and given a loving home. I will never forget Diablo. He saved me that day, and in my mind he will always be a hero.'

CHAPTER 27

MARIA AND YOGI'S STORY

The day that Maria's life changed forever started out with just another work shift as a waitress at her local pizza restaurant in Mobile, Alabama. Around 1.30 a.m. on 28 June 2015, she was on her way home when she stopped her car at a junction in an older, quiet part of Mobile with fewer street lights than other parts of town. As she sat waiting for the red lights to change, she wasn't too worried because she knew the area like the back of her hand. Maria was tired after a particularly busy shift but she was only two minutes from home so she knew that she would soon be tucked up in bed asleep.

She saw a group of eight youths walk across the road and over to her car. The boys must only have been teenagers, and Maria wondered what they were doing out so late. Four of the boys approached her car from behind and tried to open the driver's door, while the others watched.

Maria had locked the door so they couldn't get in and this seemed to make one of them very angry. Suddenly, without saying a word, he pulled a gun out and shot Maria in her face through the glass window. The bullet went through the bridge of her nose and out through the side of her face, fragmenting bones into her right eye. It all happened so quickly. Terrified, Maria hit the accelerator pedal and floored it out of there.

'No words were exchanged between me and any of the teenagers,' recalls Maria. 'They didn't ask for money or try to steal my car. I think that I was in the wrong place at the wrong time and if it hadn't been me who they shot, it would have been someone else. They were out there that night solely to shoot someone. The adrenalin must have kicked in because I didn't feel any pain at all. I didn't even panic, I just knew that I had to get out of there and get home as fast as I could. I had no idea what damage the bullet had done to my face – I just knew that I'd been shot and it was potentially serious.'

Maria's boyfriend, CJ, didn't usually stay over at her house, but this night he was waiting up for her because the next morning they were going to the beach. Maria screeched to a halt on her driveway and kept her finger on the horn. Wondering what the heck was going on, CJ ran out of the house in his boxer shorts and a tank top to find Maria bleeding and crying in the car. He rushed her to the nearest hospital.

Due to the extent of her injuries Maria was then transferred to a major trauma hospital for specialist care. The main concern was to find the bullet because the doctors were worried that it was embedded somewhere in Maria's brain.

Extensive tests and an MRI scan couldn't find it anywhere in her body – it was only later that police forensics found the bullet embedded in her car's passenger seat.

Maria was in hospital for a week, during which time she underwent two major operations. Two days after she was shot, it was evident that she couldn't see out of her right eye, so a retinal specialist was brought in from Florida to examine her. Maria's right eye was beyond repair. The bullet and bone fragments had torn through her retina, so her sight was ruined. Another doctor advised that she have this eye removed because there was a chance that, at a later date, her body might reject her good eye and she would become completely blind.

'I was on so many painkillers that week that I really wasn't very aware about what was going on,' says Maria. 'I only knew that the situation with my eye was serious and I didn't want to go completely blind. My parents, Cora and Jim, had flown in to be at my bedside with my brother, Bryan, and CJ. We collectively decided that I should have my eye removed. Everybody was so shocked by what had happened to me but a decision had to be made and, in a one-hour surgery, my eye was taken out.'

When Maria was released from hospital, she faced further problems. The day she got home with her mum, who stayed with her for the entire summer while she recuperated, there were 4 July fireworks going off until the early hours of the morning. Maria stayed curled up on the sofa the whole time, huddled in a protective blanket, with the TV on loud enough to drown out the noise that reminded her of the gun that was fired in her face. The sound of the fireworks led to horrific nightmares that prevented her from getting much-needed rest.

She couldn't settle in her own four walls because the teenagers hadn't been found yet despite a massive police manhunt. Maria was terrified that they might come back and kill her because she had survived – or, worse, harm her family in retaliation for her talking to the police. Three weeks after the attack, she moved into an apartment in another part of town for this reason.

Her story had been shared many times on local media so it seemed the whole town was on high alert until the shooter and his gang had been caught. If she went for a walk in the street, she would freeze if a car came towards her or parked near her in case it was the teenagers or their families looking for revenge.

The police found the boys several weeks later, when Maria was spending the weekend at her parents' house, and the lead detective for the case called her.

'I was so relieved and I immediately felt safer,' says Maria. 'It really was like a huge weight had been lifted from my shoulders and I could start to get on with my life. I was still very afraid and I was diagnosed with post-traumatic stress disorder but at least they were off the streets and couldn't hurt me, my family or anyone else.'

The shooter was just 15 years old and all his friends turned on him, claiming that he acted on his own and they didn't know he was going to shoot Maria. They were all sent to a juvenile detention centre.

'It was difficult for me to come to terms with what had happened,' Maria remembers. 'Of course it was devastating losing an eye but I couldn't stop thinking about how I hadn't done anything to provoke such an awful attack. I hadn't fought back, I hadn't said a word, yet the boy still shot me like I was worthless. I wasn't bitter or angry but I was incredibly upset. My life had been turned upside down because of a chance encounter. I had been due to start school to study ultrasound imaging at a local cardiology institute the week after I was shot and I had to put that on hold while I healed. It was so unfair. I would dwell on wondering what kind of a life those teenagers had where they thought it was OK to randomly shoot a person. I would get nervous just walking outside in the street because my trust in humanity was all but gone. I worried that if it could happen once, it could happen again. It was dreadful. For the first time in my life, I was afraid of the dark and my own shadow.'

Maria and CJ spent a lot of time together while she recuperated over the summer. One evening, she was browsing through Facebook when an advert posted by Mobile's Animal Rescue Foundation caught her attention. It was a picture of a tiny sandy-and-brown Border Terrier cross puppy called Bear, and he looked so pathetic because he had been injured and his left eye was damaged. The brave pup was just four weeks old and he had been brought into a local vet by his owners, who said that another dog had attacked him. His owners weren't prepared to pay his medical bills and they surrendered him to the Animal Rescue Foundation, who started a campaign to raise money for his surgery. During the operation, his vet decided that the eye, which was red and bulging out of its socket, couldn't be saved so he removed it.

The instant Maria saw the pup with one eye, she knew she had found a kindred spirit. If anyone knew what the little dog was going through, it was Maria and she wanted to help him and give him a safe, loving home.

'I showed CJ his picture and I said that I would like him,' says Maria. 'Unbeknown to me, CJ contacted the Animal Rescue Foundation and he told them my story. The next morning we went to meet Bear and I knew then that I couldn't let him spend another minute away from me. We took him home and he settled in right away. I don't think he even understood that he only had one eye because he was so young when it was taken away. As soon as I saw him and cuddled him, he snuggled up to me like he was meant to be there. I knew that, more than anybody, I could understand and help his healing.'

Maria renamed the little dog Yogi and he has blossomed under her care. He's the poster dog for other animals in need of a helping hand as part of the Animal Rescue Foundation's 'Yogi's Fund', which raises money to help pay for expensive medical bills for dogs who have been surrendered by their owners because they can't afford to pay them.

As soon as she got Yogi, Maria started to feel safe again in her own home, something she had been working on since the attack. For a small dog, Yogi's bark is so deep it sounds like a monster dog is living in the apartment, so Maria is confident that no one would even try to break in.

It didn't take long for her to venture out of the apartment regularly every day to walk Yogi because she knew that she had to do it. Yogi gave her the confidence to get out and about; though he is small, just having him by her side is like having a personal security guard. Yogi's presence makes her feel more in control because she knows that if anyone was to attack her, they would have to get through her dog first!

The pair share the same everyday problems associated with only having one eye. Neither has any depth perception so Maria can't catch a ball and Yogi has trouble getting down off the sofa or out of the car. Once, he ran after a cat and skinned his chin on the ground because he came so close to the concrete. Maria was on hand to treat his wound and give him a cuddle.

'Caring for Yogi helped me to come to terms with what happened to me,' says Maria. 'Having another living being to look after took my mind off the shooting and I felt that I had to get on with my life if I was ever going to make a difference in his. I couldn't feel sorry for myself with him around and

Life is unfair but you can't
let it define who you are

when I'd think about how unfair it all was that I was shot and I lost an eye, I'd look at him, a poor defenceless creature, and realise that he didn't ask to lose his eye either. Life is unfair but you can't let it define who you are – Yogi, who doesn't let his disability stop him doing anything, has taught me that very important lesson. My mum says she's so glad that we found each other because she believes we were meant to meet. Some days, when I'm feeling a bit down and he can sense it, Yogi will kiss my right eye socket and nuzzle beneath my chin as if to say "Mummy, it's OK". I think he genuinely knows that we're the same in many ways. We bump into things all the time but I can laugh about it now. We watch out for each other and I compensate for him all the time. My boyfriend says that together we have a full set of eyes, and it's true. Neither of us could have wished for a better match. Since I've had Yogi I feel like I'm living again. I've started my studies again and I have a future. I won't be defined by the shooting any more and while I'll never forget it and I'm still working through the PTSD, with Yogi by my side everything is a whole lot brighter.'

CHAPTER 28

KONOR AND SCOOTER'S STORY

When Konor was born to doting parents Cate and Steele, he had an uphill battle for survival.

After a worrying pregnancy in which the doctors mistakenly thought the unborn child had spina bifida, Konor was born needing multiple surgeries to repair a blocked ureter. Despite his health problems, he was a baby who slept and fed well, and who was so laid-back he barely cried or fussed. In fact, Konor was so quiet and sleepy that Cate worried there might be something wrong with her precious son. Sometimes she had to shake him to wake him up and then it would take ages for him to come round properly.

She took her son to see doctors but, as he was developing normally in all other respects, the 'experts' told her he was perfectly fine and that she should stop panicking. As a first-time mum, it was difficult for Cate to relax but, as the months went by, her fears settled down as Konor met all the milestones for his age.

She found parenting far easier when she stopped worrying so much, and Konor grew up sitting on a surfboard, being pulled around a beach in sunny California with his younger sister Makena.

They had an enviable outdoor lifestyle and Konor, who loved being in water more than anything, practically swam before he could walk. By the time he was six years old, he was taking part in local swimming competitions, which he often won. He wasn't talking as much as a child his age should, but again, doctors assured Cate that he was fine and was just developing at his own pace.

It wasn't until Konor turned nine years old that Cate's worries started to resurface and this time she knew in her heart of hearts that something was wrong with her son.

He couldn't make friends easily; when he tried, it was obvious other children didn't like him because he wasn't a 'regular' kid. Konor wasn't a team player, preferring to spend his time alone rather than mixing with children his own age. He seemed depressed and anxious most of the time and he had no self-esteem. Unlike many of his peers, he would never watch TV unless there was a documentary playing. He disliked school because he claimed the other children hated him.

'What's the point of me going to school when everyone hates me?' he often asked Cate, tears streaming down his face. 'No one wants to be my friend. I'm a joke to everyone.'

Cate would beg him to at least try to make friends but he was adamant he couldn't.

'Mum, why would I want to make friends with these people when all they do is stab me in the back?' he asked her, and his words left Cate heartbroken.

'It was painful seeing Konor fall into such a deep depression,' says Cate. 'We were at our wits' end. How was it possible that a healthy young boy could be so unhappy? He had a wonderful, stable home life. We had given him every opportunity imaginable to do what interested him and yet he had few social skills and no friends. Konor would often have temper tantrums and scream that nobody cared about him. He'd get frustrated with me, with his family, with everything in his life. As his mother, I instinctively knew that something serious was wrong with him. This wasn't just a phase.'

Konor was bullied at school and he would get to school early so that he could hide in the bathrooms until the first bell went. When the children picked their sports teams, he would be the last one standing every time, even though he was very athletic and would have been a great asset to any team. Konor felt this alienation acutely and, even though he was picked on by the other boys, he desperately wanted a friend – yet he didn't know how to behave around them.

Cate moved him to different schools several times but each time it was the same scenario: Konor was frustrated because no one wanted to know him. On the rare occasions he did make a connection, the friendships didn't last long once they got to know him and his quirks. He was often blocked by his 'friends' on Facebook, which upset Konor more than anything, or they would arrange to come over to hang out and never show up, without so much as a phone call or an explanation. Konor associated friendship with profound emotional pain, so he became even more withdrawn and unhappy, choosing to stay in his room for hours on end and to eat

How was it possible that a healthy young boy could be so unhappy?

when he felt like it, not at mealtimes with his family. Cate could feel the pain he was in and she just didn't know what to do to help.

He developed strange, obsessive habits which baffled Cate. Whenever songs came on the radio with high-pitched female voices, he would hold his hands over his ears as if the music hurt them. Konor had to wear sports shorts under everything, even his jeans when he went to school, and he was very selective as to the kinds of clothes he could wear on any given day. It was like he had a pattern that he couldn't ever change.

Eventually, he was diagnosed with Asperger's syndrome, a condition similar to autism but often with more severe and far-reaching symptoms. Children with Asperger's typically experience social-skill problems and communication difficulties, and display eccentric, repetitive behavioural rituals. Konor was also diagnosed with attention deficit hyperactivity disorder (ADHD), a common mental health condition where the sufferer has problems with focus and is often unable to control their impulses. Konor was exhibiting most of the symptoms of Asperger's and, while it was helpful to have a diagnosis, dealing with his symptoms was a daily struggle for his family.

Throughout the turmoil in Konor's life, there was one constant: his Maltese dog Scooter. Scooter was adopted by the family when Konor was nine. When Cate found Scooter, he was just four days old and she bottle-fed him for the next eight weeks. Scooter's original owner was a woman who had bred the puppies to pay for her honeymoon but she couldn't cope with them all and had asked Cate to take care of Scooter.

As Konor grew older and his issues became more apparent, Cate realised that the little dog was helping her son. One of Konor's extreme fears was of the dark. He had always been terrified of being alone at night and he would have vivid nightmares of fire-breathing dragons and fierce dinosaurs chasing and attacking him. Cate bought a sofa and put it in Konor's room next to his bed. Scooter soon started to sleep here and Konor's nightmares became far less frequent. Sometimes Cate would go into his room to get him up and he would be snuggled up with Scooter on the sofa after he had woken up in the night following a bad dream. The difference now was that, rather than panicking and screaming for his parents in the early hours of the morning, if Konor woke up he had Scooter to reassure him.

Konor's anguish at having few friends was also lessened by Scooter. The little dog would follow him all over the house and play with him in the garden, so he had less time and energy to feel lonely. They could never fall out because, unlike a human, Scooter was never cross with Konor and he could never hurt his feelings. Scooter loved him unconditionally.

As Konor grew older and became a teenager, he was angry much of the time and he had a different concept of personal space to most people. He would punch Cate in the guts 'just because', or he would kick her in the hamstrings because he thought it was funny or he was having a particularly bad day. When he was furious, he would scream and cry and throw things around. Tiny Scooter taught him self-control because Konor knew he had to be gentle with him and he didn't want to scare him.

'It was interesting because as soon as Konor would get angry, rather than being afraid, Scooter would go running to him,' says Cate. 'Just seeing a friendly face was often enough to defuse the situation significantly. Often Konor would sit down with Scooter on his lap and, rather than talk to me or his dad about his feelings or problems, he would tell Scooter who would, of course, be all ears and non-judgemental. You could see the tension literally disappearing from Konor's face as he patted his dog and

 You could see the tension literally disappearing from Konor's face

cuddled him close to his face. A lick and a snuggle from Scooter meant more to him than anything I could ever say or do. I think that engaging with his dog also helped him to eventually find it easier to talk to me and his dad. Telling Scooter his innermost secrets made him realise that it was OK to talk about problems and fears; that it was actually a good thing because he didn't feel so alone.'

Scooter also gave Konor responsibilities that he took very seriously. Taking him for walks was crucial to Konor and the act of getting out of the house helped his mood swings. He even started to interact with other people walking their dogs in the park; talking to strangers was something he had never done before. Scooter gave him a sense of security and a belief that he was worth speaking to.

From an early age, Konor had shown great promise in sports. When Scooter came into his life, he started to compete in triathlons, where he took part in bike races, swimming competitions and running races, usually over the course of a weekend. Thanks to Scooter, Konor was able to excel at his sport as they would often train together in the park, or the dog would accompany him to competitions, staying with him right up until the start of the race, keeping him calm and focused.

Now Konor is recognised as a huge talent on the San Diego triathlete circuit, with sponsorship from an adult team called Breakaway Training, and his ambition is to win an Ironman competition. He has made many new friends through his chosen sport and, for the first time in his life, he's popular with his peers and adults alike – something he never would have thought possible when he was growing up.

Konor is also in demand as a public speaker because he gives inspiring talks to schoolchildren and youth groups to show them that even with learning difficulties and disabilities, anyone can lead a fulfilling life. Scooter is ever present and helps the young man relax and focus on his presentations. With him, Konor has no fear.

'I don't believe that Konor would be where he is in his life if he didn't have Scooter,' says Cate. 'He has done more for my son than all the doctors in the world could ever do. He has taught him so much about himself. Scooter has made him accept many things about his life: that he can't please everyone; that it's OK for people not to like him because Scooter will love him no matter what. Scooter will always be his calm when he's in the middle of a storm, whether that's a temper tantrum, anxiety or an upset. He knows that he will always be there to help and comfort him no matter what the situation. Truly, we didn't save Scooter – he saved us.'

After witnessing the amazing transformation Scooter has caused in Konor, Cate now runs a charity called Shelter Dogs to Dream Dogs. She takes in unwanted dogs who might otherwise be destroyed and pairs them with candidates who

Scooter will always be his calm when he's in the middle of a storm

need reliable companions to assist them in their day-to-day lives. Cate meticulously trains her dogs to a person's specific needs and has achieved huge success in pairing dogs with owners.

'In Scooter I saw that shelter pets can do so much more than we give them credit for,' says Cate. 'He turned out to be the most loyal companion, the best antidote to my son's issues. I realised that if he could make such a difference, then so could other unwanted pets. They deserved a chance as much as the next dog. Konor and my daughter Makena also help me train the dogs, so it's become a family affair. It's something we feel passionate about and, with hard work and dedication, it really works. It's a win–win situation. We rescue the dogs and they in turn rescue their new owners in all manner of different ways. Scooter really proved that dogs like him are worth their weight in gold.'

AFTERWORD

Throughout the interview and research process for this book, and from my own family's personal experiences, it has been abundantly clear to me that, if only given the chance, rescue dogs can establish profound connections with their human owners and have a huge impact on their lives. This wide-ranging collection of stories demonstrates, often in the most unexpected ways, that the decision to get a rescue dog is life-changing – and may even turn out to be life-saving.

The intelligence and acute 'sixth-sense' awareness of these canines in detecting and responding to physical, mental and emotional distress in their owners are undeniable. Rescue dogs are often prejudged and pigeonholed as inferior animals with baggage, when their unfortunate starts in life may in fact lead to an increased sensitivity to pain and trauma, and to an even greater capacity for support, loyalty and love.

I hope that *My Rescue Dog Rescued Me* will help to raise the profile and value of shelter dogs, and that more unlucky canines will be paired with the right humans to find their forever homes. So, please seriously consider adopting, not shopping for, your next dog – it might well be the best decision of your life.

#AdoptDontShop

RESCUE DOG RESOURCES

While researching this book, I was staggered to discover just how many rescue dog groups there are around the world and particularly in the UK. Here is a selection of rescue dog charities and organisations that I hope you will find helpful as a starting point if you have been inspired by this collection of stories to adopt your very own rescue dog.

Adore-a-Bull Rescue – www.adoreabull.org

American Society for the Prevention of Cruelty to Animals (ASPCA) – www.aspca.org

Battersea Dogs and Cats Home – www.battersea.org.uk

Dogs for Good (previously Dogs for the Disabled) – www.dogsforgood.org

Dog Rescue Pages – www.dogpages.org.uk

Gentle Giants Rescue – www.gentlegiantsrescue.com

Humane Society International – www.hsi.org

Humane Society of the United States –
www.humanesociety.org

Lanta Animal Welfare – www.lantaanimalwelfare.com

Medical Detection Dogs –
www.medicaldetectiondogs.org.uk

Petfinder – www.petfinder.com

Pets for Homes – www.pets4homes.co.uk

Rescue Me! – www.rescueme.org

Royal Society for the Prevention of Cruelty to Animals
(RSPCA) – www.rspca.org.uk

Shelter Dogs to Dream Dogs –
www.shelterdogstodreamdogs.com

Soi Dog Foundation – www.soidog.org

South Lake Animal League – www.slal.org

Spanish Stray Dogs UK – www.spanishstraydogs.org.uk

UK Dog Rescue Group Directory –
www.dog.rescueshelter.com/uk

War Dogs Making it Home –
www.wardogsmakingithome.org

ACKNOWLEDGEMENTS

Thank you to all the rescue dog owners who have generously shared their stories for this book. I have enjoyed every minute listening to your heart-warming and inspirational tales.

And thank you to the rescue groups who kindly put me in touch with these wonderful people and families. You have so many success stories to talk about and this is testament to your profound love for dogs and the extraordinary lengths you go to in order to find them homes.

The dog owners and rescue groups alike have restored my faith in human nature and I'm grateful for the opportunity to share their experiences with the world.

Finally, thanks to my own little shelter dogs, Alfie and Beau, who will forever have a piece of my heart for always being there for me and my family. We love you both!